Centre for Research
on Canadian-Russian Relations
at Carleton University

Slavic Research Group
at University of Ottawa

CANADA/RUSSIA SERIES

Volume 6

General Editors
J.L. Black
Andrew Donskov

CRCR

Naomi Ziman Roberts and Peter M. Roberts, 1957.

To dear Ann with many memories of some shared experiencies. Love from Naomi

FIRST FOREIGN POSTING

12 Nov. 2005

MOSCOW 1957-1959

Letters to the Family

Naomi Ziman Roberts
& Peter M. Roberts

PENUMBRA PRESS
www.penumbrapress.ca

LIBRARY AND ARCHIVES CANADA CATALOGUING IN PUBLICATION
Roberts, Naomi Ziman, 1929-
        First foreign posting : Moscow 1957-1959 / Naomi Ziman Roberts &
Peter M. Roberts.
(Canada/Russia series ; 6) Co-published by the Centre for Research on Canadian-Russian
Relations, Carleton University.
ISBN 1-894131-79-7
        1. Roberts, Naomi Ziman, 1929- --Correspondence. 2. Roberts, Peter, 1927-2003. 3.
Moscow (Russia)--Description and travel. 4. Diplomats' spouses--Russia (Federation)--
Moscow--Correspondence. 5. Diplomats' spouses--Canada--Correspondence. I. Roberts,
Peter, 1927-2003 II. Carleton University. Centre for Research on Canadian-Russian
Relations. III. Title. IV. Series.
FC636.R62A4 2005   914.7'3104852   C2005-902937-4

Canada

Penumbra Press gratefully acknowledges the financial support of the Government of
Canada through the Book Publishing Industry Development Program (BPIDP) for our
publishing activities. We also acknowledge the Government of Ontario through the
Ontario Media Development Corporation's Ontario Book Initiative.

For our children, Frances and Jeremy Roberts,
and for their children
Jeremy, Derek, and Mark Smith
Jane, Jasmine, and Jacob Roberts

ACKNOWLEDGEMENTS

I appreciate the generosity of certain former Moscow associates who kindly allowed me to borrow and to reproduce some of their personal snapshots. Thank you to all of them.

I am indebted also to Mag Carson of Penumbra Press, who has created a fine photo display and a striking cover design for this book.

PREFACE

During a summer spent in London in 1993 I helped to sort and dispose of the extensive archive in my late parents' home. Among the accumulated items I found two plastic bags containing the letters that Peter Roberts and I had sent to the London-based relatives during Peter's posting in Moscow from September 1957 to September 1959. (Unfortunately, the many letters which Peter had written to his family in Canada were not preserved.) I brought the London letters home to Ottawa and re-read them with amusement and amazement.

Nearly a decade later the president of Penumbra Press, John Flood, learning by chance that I had this cache of letters written more than forty years earlier, surprised me with a telephone call and a request to see a sample of the letters. I dipped into the plastic bags and typed up some pages for his consideration. He expressed a serious interest, and with his encouragement I set about preparing the remaining letters (an exercise that continued, with many pauses, for nearly two years). The result is the present volume.

Peter Roberts died in 2003, following a protracted illness. He was not well enough to be involved in the preparation of the book, but he did know that it was likely that our letters would be published, and he gave his approval in principle to the project. Like me, he had enjoyed re-discovering his younger self as he read the letters that we had written so long ago. But he had no hand in the editing of the text, for which I must take responsibility.

The editing consists mainly of the elimination of some material too trivial to interest any reader today; perhaps I should have excluded more on these grounds. Conversely, a small amount of fresh material has been added, incorporated (I hope seamlessly) into the original text. This was done partly in order to avoid the use of footnotes where a meaning was not clear. More significantly, a few anecdotes have been added that were not included in a letter but remain in my memory and were probably shared with family during time spent together. It is to be hoped that this minor post facto editorial tampering does not affect the spontaneity of the whole.

At the end of the book will be found some biographical notes concerning the subsequent professional activities of people whose names most frequently occur in these letters. In some cases we remained in touch long after the Moscow connection had ceased, but in other cases I have had to rely on public sources for my information, and these notes are therefore sketchy at best.

As readers will soon discover, the letters reproduced in this book are personal in nature, and I was initially ambivalent about making the correspondence public. But John Flood's enthusiasm reassured me, and convinced me that I should go ahead with the project. I am grateful to him for the confidence he has shown, and I hope that others will share his pleasure in reading this week-by-week account of two eventful years spent in the Soviet Union during the Cold War.

— Naomi Roberts

Moscow,
Aug. 30 1959.

My dear Ma, Pa, Liz,

The week has consisted of one

Moscow,
May 9, 1958.

Letters to the Family

Moscow

My dear parents & Liz

8 April 1958

Dear Everybody,
I have only just heard that there is a bag leaving
today, so this won't be the long letter you were all hoping for.
From now on, I believe, the bag will be leaving every Monday, not
Wednesday, as formerly. This week things are odd because of Easter.

We had a wonderful holiday and both feel so much
better for it. I didn't realize how the strain was accumulating
until we got outside the Curtain, when suddenly all one's troubles
slipped away and the world looked quite a miserable place. Not
that life here is at all bad, but everyone agrees that it is important to get out for a few days at least, every 6 months if possible. If one is not to become too irritable and I am proud to
both come back rosy-cheeked and full of energy [to-say 'my statistics: 34.26,
announce that thanks to all my whizzing around London I have lost
one inch in each of the vital places look like fashionable sacks. Which
36] and all my skin tight dresses within the Soviet Union. Now
we are busy planning various trips meanwhile, I am admitted to 8 socks in the blade-
should be fun. starting next Monday.

My dear Parents and Liz,

How strange it all is. The Russians look so very Russian. I suppose I should not be surprised.

We have exchanged friendly words with the young man we correctly identified as belonging to the British Embassy (he is the new Third Secretary) and with a French girl he has in tow who is to be a guest of the British Ambassador. Also with a tubby, soft-spoken Brigadier Young, the British Military Attaché. And with Lady Blake, who is to be the guest of the British Naval Attaché (it was she who was bidding the schoolboys goodbye at the dock). We have *not*, however, talked with the man we heard introducing himself to some Russians as the Moscow *Daily Worker* correspondent.

Our table companions are a Finnish Lutheran minister, very young, and a Finnish girl student who is returning after a three-month stint as a ward-maid in a London hospital. Neither speaks English with any confidence and we don't talk much at table. The meals are so horrible that we hustle through them as fast as we can. Much the best dish so far was a raw apple. I think we will lay in a private stock of food in Copenhagen.

Unlike our friends the Cunard line, this *passagierskaya liniya* does not try to provide distraction for its passengers, in fact one has a hard job ever to locate a crew member except at meals, for which the waitress rounds us up punctually at the appointed hour with ferocious commands to "sit down please."

Our stewardess, however, is a very jolly girl who, when addressed, puts down anything she is holding, places her feet wide apart and her hands on her ribs below her bosom, and talks without pause until her audience departs. Peter's Russian seems entirely adequate, much to his delight.

The only concession to passenger entertainment is piped music in all the public rooms, and in the cabins too if the equipment is not unplugged. (I gather this is very common in the Soviet Union.) The music is mainly old German songs (including "Auf Wiedersehen," for which I have a sentimental attachment stemming from a holiday in Austria a lifetime ago) or Rock and Roll, and it is noisy and disagreeable.

This morning the sea was rough and we felt a little queasy, but this evening it is calm again. There is a shuffleboard court painted on the deck, but needless to say no disks or paddles to play with. However, we found some rope quoits and used one to play a game of deck tennis over

an imaginary net. Later the young Englishman and his French companion joined us and they put up an ingenious net made of deck chairs. Soon
an audience collected to watch the British at their sport. It was quite fun.

So much to tell that I haven't taken breath to express our appreciation
of the all-too-short (for us) holiday. You were all three most considerate of
our wishes both to do and not to do, and I don't know when I have
enjoyed a week more. May there be many more like it. I hated to see you
disappear round the immigration shed, but we will not be so far away as
we were in Ottawa.

By the way, Peter collected his Simpson's parcel from the Purser (or, as
he is called in Russian, the "passenger helper," though he looks too sinister to merit such a title), so we need not worry about writing angry letters
to anyone.

I don't know how we will buy Danish stamps with English money late
on a Sunday night, but if we are able to do so I will mail this letter to you
in Copenhagen.

For now, goodbye and best thanks for a lovely holiday. We have been
repeating to one another with much merriment passages from *At the Drop
of a Hat*. Thanks for that memorable evening.

Your affectionate
Naomi

—— ——

Moscow
1 October 1957

My dear Parents and Liz,

Diplomatic bag leaves on Wednesday, so I had better start on a letter,
even though I do not yet feel in a position to make any inspired comments
on the Moscow scene. It is in most ways very much as I had imagined, people dressed shabbily and looking like the picture-book Russians with black
moustaches and flashing eyes — some of them, at least, from the south-
eastern part probably. Buildings: new ones either very frilly or very severe,
apartment blocks quite shoddily built; old buildings crumbling to pieces
but still very much lived in, and often rather handsome. The Embassy is of
the crumbling type, especially the house in which we are now staying,
which is apart from the main building though within the Embassy compound. This is the Counsellor's apartment, really a large family home on
two floors. The new Counsellor is expected in December, complete with
wife and four children. Meanwhile our own apartment, occupying part of
the main floor of the Embassy proper, is being repainted and cleaned and

generally spruced up, and none too soon. The kitchen and bathroom are particularly squalid.

Today I went to the market with Kris, the Second Secretary's wife (he is Vic Moore), the only other External Affairs wife until the Crowe family arrives. Kris was previously married and has a six-year-old son and another baby on the way. It was fun in the market, though one is very much the centre of attention. The Russians are quite unabashed and crowd up close, jostle, and even pinch us to see whether we are flesh and blood. Mostly they have pleasant expressions, but occasionally we see one looking really nasty, and doubtless hoping to catch us out doing something unlawful.

Our other Russian experience so far (apart from walks and car rides) was an afternoon at the circus last Sunday. The place was full of children and grandmothers, the latter all wearing their uniform head scarves, even though it was very hot. We had an extra ticket (we had been given three by someone who could not use them), so we invited Nikolai, one of the Embassy drivers, and he bought us ice cream cones, which were excellent. Nikolai is thrilled to have a Russian-speaking passenger, and he talks to Peter constantly. What he says is sensible enough, but he cuts in when Peter and I are talking to one another as if English speech were non-speech. I get a little annoyed, but obviously there is only one thing to do, namely to learn to speak Russian. It is quite maddening not to be able to communicate, and I am sure I will be able to enjoy it all much more when I am reasonably fluent.

I am going to be writing long frequent letters to the Roberts family, as Peter will not have the time to do so; therefore I think I will start making carbon copies of letters of a general nature, and will add private bits to individual letters.

In answer to Pa's question, I understand that both the newspapermen you mentioned have left already; people do not stay very long in Moscow. Doubtless we will meet others of your friends and acquaintances as we get around; we will mention the names of likely people among those whose acquaintance we make and you can tell us if you know them.

Did you get my letter posted in Copenhagen?

Later: I am sending a typed general letter with this. More next week.

Thanks again for a lovely holiday, which I suspect I shall be looking back upon wistfully in the months to come.

Much love,

N.

P.S. Please will you keep my letters in case I ever want to re-read them?

Moscow
3 October 1957

Dear Lethbridge Family,
Dear London Family,

I can hardly believe we've been here only five days. Each day is so full and so new that it must surely count as a week.

But to go back to the voyage. I think we have already told you about the boat and our fellow-passengers, so I'll tell you now about the stops we made.

The first stop was in Copenhagen, where we arrived about 6:00 p.m. and spent the night there — or rather the boat did. It was a beautiful evening and we prowled the streets for hours and were delighted with the buildings. We had an excellent meal with very pleasant service — which one notices after a few days on the *Baltika*. After dinner Peter of course wanted to embark upon a sociological study of the nightspots. We followed a group of young men into an upstairs room somewhere; I don't know what Peter expected of them, but certainly not what we got, namely a poetry-reading in Danish (a recital of their own works, I think). We made a hasty exit, red-faced, as soon as a break occurred. Later, Peter spotted a Canadian sailor entering a dingy bar and insisted we follow him. Luckily for me the bar closed at midnight and we were thrown out. We returned to the boat, rather cross with one another.

Our next stop was Stockholm, which is bigger and probably more interesting for a long stay, but at first sight not so attractive, especially as it poured relentlessly during our afternoon there. No taxis to be had, so we made our way by bus to the Canadian Embassy, but there seemed to be no one at home. This is hard to believe, so I can only think that we didn't find the right place; the building was undergoing repair, and there were no notices pinned on it to help poor strangers. So we gave up and walked in the rain till we came to Nordiska, the big department store. Here we spent an hour browsing, then went to a posh place to have dinner. As we were in Sweden I said we had to have smorgasbord, but it was a mistake, just bits of cold ham and lettuce, etc., and expensive too.

In Helsinki we were luckier. Peter telephoned an acquaintance at the Embassy, and as their bag had just closed they were all relaxing (just as one used to do after the weekly tutorial). The two Embassy stenographers were assigned to accompany us in the Embassy car on a tour of the town. This was the best way of seeing it, as it was a very cold day with a bitter wind, quite common in Helsinki, they told us. The town is very hilly, with lots of water and lots of trees, and some very handsome houses. The Chargé kindly invited us to his apartment for dinner, where we met his wife and two small girls. (His name is Orme Dier.)

We went back to the ship at ten and started on the last lap at six the next morning.

We disembarked at Leningrad at eight on Thursday. There was a gorgeous muddle and confusion, with too few Intourist officials looking after too many passengers (who could have managed quite easily by themselves but weren't allowed to). I benefited slightly from the confusion, for they sent off half our luggage to the wrong hotel, and while Peter was telephoning Moscow I was whisked off in a taxi to retrieve it, and so had a short tour of the city. I thought the buildings remarkably handsome — all pre-Revolutionary — and the streets broad and splendid. Finally our affairs were sorted out, we were allowed to buy train tickets, we were presented with a phenomenal bill by Intourist (about $30 for getting us and seven very light bags from the docks to the station via the hotel) and at midnight we shut ourselves in our compartment, which was quite adequate, though I can't say the same for the public washroom.

Moscow arrived next morning before we expected it, and at first we thought the bunch of shacks was a railway siding, not the main station of the great capital. However, here were Vic and Len to meet us, and we had to re-pack in a great hurry. (A British couple we later met told me that they made the same mistake, and greeted their welcoming First Secretary in their pyjamas.)

That day and the next were pretty depressing. The Houzer family (whom we replace) had all been ill, everything was in chaos, and the apartment was a mess. We are being put up temporarily in the Counsellor's apartment (he won't arrive until December) and, oh joy, I learned yesterday that our own apartment is going to be re-painted and generally spruced up before we move in. It has great potential, and all the rooms are lovely except the kitchen and bathroom, which are frights. Even these are capable of being improved, however. The apartment has two bedrooms and will feel spacious to us, accustomed as we are to tiny one-bedroom spaces in Ottawa. But the Houzers must have felt cramped, for they have two young children with them, with all the paraphernalia that small children require.

Well, on Friday morning we had lunch with the Ambassador, who lives above the offices in a very handsome apartment, huge rooms with fine chandeliers. Also present were Len and Edie Houzer (now departed from Moscow) and Vic and Kris Moore. Vic is Second Secretary and Kris is his wife of five months, a Swede with a six-year-old son from a previous marriage. The Moores live in a diplomatic block of flats half an hour's drive away. On the evening of the same day the Moores gave a farewell party for the Houzers, to which we were invited. There were thirty-two guests, all fairly young, and those we spoke to seemed nice. All were diplomats or children of diplomats, or journalists. It was a buffet dinner, and "informal," as the expression goes.

On Saturday we had lunch with the Military Attaché, Ken Campbell, and we made our own dinner out of food from the Houzers' fridge. On Sunday we saw the Houzers off at the airport (where there is still a statue of Stalin in evidence), and in the afternoon went to the circus with tickets given to us by the Moores. It was very good.

On Monday my assigned maid did not turn up, and since neither our food order nor the extra baggage we sent on from London nor the stuff we had sent "ahead" from Ottawa had arrived, and we were told that the latter would take months yet, most likely, I felt pretty low. However, the maid business is now straightened out, and it seems likely that she will be a very good cook, and we have made up our minds that *our* stuff will come from Ottawa very quickly, never mind what other people's experiences have been. Peter has sent a telegram to Ottawa urging them on.

Of course my great trouble is that I do not speak Russian, and very maddening it is. Today I went shopping by myself to buy Peter some tobacco and felt delirious with triumph when I emerged from the shop with my purchase. I must have used all of a dozen words. On the way back I stopped to gaze in the shop windows, and the passersby stopped to gaze at me. I am told that one soon gets used to being the zoo animal on display, but I find it quite alarming when they crowd up close to get a better view, and follow me from stall to stall in the market in order not to miss any of the fun.

I'll tell you more next week; the bag leaves shortly and I don't want to miss it. Both sets of parents are getting copies of this letter, as are Mary and Liz.

Much love to all,
Ever,
Naomi

—◆◆—

Moscow
7 October 1957

Dear Parents and Liz,
Dear Mother and Father Roberts and Mary,

I'll get started on Letter no. 2 from Moscow today, in case I am prevented from writing much tomorrow. At the moment we have the only "home" on the compound (other than the residences of the Ambassador and the Security Guards), and this means that any stray member of the Canadian community with an hour to put in around the Embassy drops in here. In many ways this is nice for me, but it does mean that I sometimes have to rearrange my day's timetable at short notice.

Well, the week's events. On Wednesday night we were given complimentary tickets to go to a theatre in order to watch some Indonesians performing Indonesian songs and dances. There were one or two quite interesting dances, especially one that portrayed two men wrestling, but by halftime we had had enough and sneaked out.

The prelude to the performance was quite an eye-opener. Four Indonesians in native costume stood in front of the curtain on the right and four stalwart Russians on the left, each clasping a bunch of flowers. I forget at which stage the bouquets changed hands. There were welcoming speeches on the subject of Russian-Indonesian friendship, together with translations of the Indonesian bits, for exactly half an hour, followed by the national anthems (very long) of both countries. Both before and during the performance photographers turned hot bright arc lights on the distinguished part of the audience, namely us, which was unpleasant and hard on the eyes. We recognized Mikoyan in a private box, and he very wisely ducked behind a curtain when the light was spotted on him. At one point during the performance a photographer succeeded in fusing all the lights, stage ones included. We sat in pitchy blackness for about ten minutes, hoping there would not be a panic, but the Russian part of the audience behaved just like any audience and clapped and laughed derisively. I thought this a healthy sign. Another unplanned incident occurred when one of the speech-making Indonesians was making his exit and got caught up in the curtain. The theatre itself was rather pretty, though the seats were uncomfortable.

People tell us that the improvement in goods displayed in the shops and in things people wear is noticeable not only year by year but actually week by week. Whenever there is anything new offered for sale, even luxury items like cut-glass vases, there is always a queue — or more often a surge — of struggling, elbowing, would-be buyers. The other day when we went into a shop that sold nothing but maps we got lifted right off our feet by the mass of people who also wanted to buy maps. (They were not city maps, such as we have looked for in vain.)

I've seen a lot of badly mutilated or scarred people, mainly around the market, who look horribly poor, with their stumps of leg or arm wrapped around in sackcloth; but on the other hand I've seen quite a lot of people warmly wrapped in a decent coat and matching hat. The children look healthy and happy, the little ones already bundled to the eyes in layer after layer of coats, woollies, and scarves. The young women workers, sweeping streets or building houses, all wear baggy blue cotton trousers tucked into mannish socks, and padded cotton jackets. They look every bit as tough as the men, sturdy legs and broad shoulders, and they'd need to, too, given the work they do. I understand that most women work an eight-hour day (often manual labour), queue for food for a couple of hours, then struggle home to feed the family.

But I was telling you about our week. On Friday I went with a couple of the male clerks (i.e., security guards — they mainly work nights) to GUM, the immense government-run department store, and poked around there without being tempted to buy anything. The store is made up of a series of arcades, with hundreds of individual shops facing the covered passage-ways. There are, I think, four arcades, each of them four storeys high, so you see "hundreds" is not an exaggeration. Each shop offers a specialty, but the choice seems very limited. For example, in the hat shop a cus-tomer-saleswoman dialogue might go like this: "I want a hat." "Large or small?" "Large." "Black or brown?" "Brown." "Here it is." It was an enjoy-able excursion, all the same.

Also on Friday our suitcases that were in the hold of the *Baltika* arrived. And we have news today that there is something in Customs waiting for us to claim it, which we hope is the cases of white port from London, or else our food order from Copenhagen. Also, Ottawa cabled us that our main luggage should by now be in Helsinki, so almost within shouting dis-tance. Good.

On Saturday Peter and I travelled on the Metro, which is most impres-sive, very clean and fast. A gang of sweepers, mostly women, is at work constantly, and I gather you are in big trouble if you drop so much as a ticket stub on the ground. On the other hand, in the street people spit vig-orously, so I need to skip nimbly in order to avoid becoming the spittoon. (Don't imagine as a result of some of my comments that we are not well and comfortable; we are. The blacker side of the picture is more fun to describe than the brighter side, so remember that my letters may not always be truly balanced.) Speaking of pictures, we popped into an art show while waiting for the map shop to open on Saturday. All the pictures were characteristic examples of Soviet realism, though some showed quite a daring use of colour and design. The sculptures and the portraits were more pleasing, conventional but agreeable.

Sunday we spent pleasantly alone and on Monday our social life began and promises to continue all this week. Today we go to our first dinner party, at our own Ambassador's (therefore a "working" occasion), and yesterday we went to our first cocktail party, as guests of the British Ambassador. The British Embassy is quite lovely, with great open fireplaces surrounded by carved woodwork, elaborate plaster work on the ceilings, fine chandeliers, and beautiful floors made of many different woods in a formal pattern. It also offers a stunning view across the river to the Kremlin. We conversed with dozens of people, some pretty formidable but others more promising. This party seemed to be mostly for high-ups in the diplomatic corps, and I think we must owe our invitation to one of our travelling companions from the *Baltika*, perhaps Lady Blake, whom I like immensely. Perhaps not, though; possibly we would have been invited anyway, as newcomers. *Ya niznaiyoo.* ("I don't know" — a very useful phrase.)

This brings you up to date, and I must go and change for the Ambassador's party. I shall do as last week and send copies all round to the two families, but please turn over for a personal note, which I shall add to each of you.

I hope you are all well and will keep on writing to us.

Much love from us both,

Ever,

Naomi

—◦—

Moscow

15 October 1957

Dear Parents and Liz

Dear Mother and Father Roberts and Mary

Here I come with letter no. 3. I wonder whether you like being addressed collectively? Probably I shall have your reaction to my first Moscow letter on Saturday, and you can lodge complaints then (and later) if you disapprove of the system. But if I were to write to each of you individually I suspect you would hear from me less frequently and at less length, so I hope very much that you don't mind it this way. f…

My diary doesn't tell me much this week, and indeed I have been pretty idle. I haven't yet settled down to having a servant, and I find that today, when Nina is away sick, my spirits are abnormally high, just because I've got the place to myself and too much to do. Nina is a pretty good cook and reasonably good at cleaning (I hire her now both as maid and as cook), but she is inclined to be temperamental. She gets very impatient with me for not understanding her Russian, and I am looking forward to the day when I can talk right back to her in her own tongue. Unfortunately, the mechanics of living in Moscow as a foreigner are too complex to allow one to do without a servant of any kind, and there is no such thing as a part-time servant to be hired from *Burobin*, and we are not allowed to obtain help other than through *Burobin*. Well, I expect I shall become all too dependent on servants before I am through.

On Tuesday of last week we attended our first dinner; it was at our own Ambassador's, where the Canadians are expected to be sub-hosts and sub-hostesses. The eating part was pretty good, but the talking part less so (at least so far as I was concerned).

Our second dinner party, to which we went last night, was on the other hand very pleasant conversation-wise. The host was the Belgian Ambassador, and we had been told that the Belgians were renowned as having the best table in Moscow. I think I once had a meal to compare with this one, when I was in France, but Peter claims that he has never, ever eaten a meal like it, and I can well believe it. They fly in the ingredients for a party meal fresh from Stockholm, but that alone is certainly not the secret. First we had a small portion of the most delicious soup, and this was followed by endives wrapped in ham in a sauce that I certainly could not analyze. The main course was hare, served with potato balls, chestnut stuffing, and an again indescribable sauce. Then we had some sort of creamy pudding in a flan shell. Although the guests helped themselves from dishes held by the maids, the pieces had already been carved (the hare) or cut (the flan) and the portions were quite small, so that one did not feel at all stuffed by the end of the meal — in fact I could happily have gone back over the whole thing again. One is offered a second helping of each course, but I am too afraid of being left behind to dare to accept. The wines and champagne were as good as the food, and so were the coffee and the brandy and liqueurs. So altogether we don't mind if we are invited by the Belgians quite often. Our fellow guests (we were twenty-two in all) were of various nationalities and mostly of high rank. The Belgians don't mind mixing Third Secretaries and Ambassadors, as some missions do. Mostly French was spoken, though some English and German too, and after struggling with Russian for a couple of weeks I felt blissfully fluent in French. One of my neighbours at dinner was telling me of his exploits in the French Resistance throughout the war, then turned to chat with the German Ambassador, with whom he was clearly on the best of terms. Funny how quickly and smoothly these re-alliances have taken place.

In between these two dinner-parties we have had lunch with our own Ambassador (really a Men's Lunch, but the guest failed to arrive and I was invited to come and eat his share), and we have attended a quite pleasant and informal cocktail party given by one of the British Third Secretaries to welcome another one, John Ure, with whom we travelled on the *Baltika*.

On Saturday we walked in the town (again darting to avoid the spittle and steering round the people, women as well as men, who blow their noses without the aid of a handkerchief) and poked around the odd bookshop and store. As usual the streets and shops were crowded like a Christmas rush, but I am beginning to get the hang of the shopping situation. For every person buying something I think another ten are watching him buy it — just for something to do. Also, a shortage of sales clerks tends to hold things up. For example in the shoe department we watched them let in one customer at a time to sit on the one chair while he tried on shoes; meanwhile the other customers queued patiently behind a barrier and watched the one inside. But in the food stores it is quite different; everybody is buying and things move fast. The staff who touch the food don't handle the money at all (a very good thing as regards hygiene). First one has to establish the cost of what one wants to buy, after it has been weighed, then one has to go to the cash desk and obtain a chit confirming that one has paid this amount, then one returns to the counter and exchanges the chit for the package of food. This means the purchaser has to queue three times, in addition to the first queue outside while waiting for the shop to open. As you will have guessed, this is one of the reasons we employ servants. But I must say that all the food we have bought here has been very good, especially the bread, which is nutritious and excellent, and some tasty ham we bought yesterday by the method I have just described. (We are living almost totally "Russian" until our food order from Copenhagen arrives.)

On Sunday Peter and I and three of "the girls" (stenos and clerks) were driven out in an Embassy car some sixty kilometres from Moscow in order to visit Tchaikovsky's house, now a museum. (The Ambassador makes a point of arranging treats like this for the benefit of the office staff; I would think that is quite unusual among heads of mission.) The house was quite pleasant, full of the usual assembled bits and pieces of the famous dead — including his medicine bottles and a box of liver pills from a chemist at Piccadilly Circus — and the lady guide was very sweet and enthusiastic. Mr Roberts kindly interpreted. At the end the guide played us some Tchaikovsky records on a good hi-fi. The garden was nice, but nicest of all was just being in the country. The Embassy driver brought his daughter along, a girl of twenty, a keen member of the Communist Youth Organization and quite sophisticated. The poor girl had got all dressed up for the excursion in her North American clothes (the local staff are allowed to put in a $50.00 order to Eaton's every year), and the rest of us turned up for our country outing looking like a bunch of slobs.

Yesterday, it being Canadian Thanksgiving Day, Peter stayed home and read his papers, and in the afternoon we went for a walk. We get far too little exercise and fresh air, so I feel that when it is not too bitter we should walk all we can at the weekends. We have already had some pretty cold weather, but Monday was comparatively mild.

You are now up to date on our activities. Also it is lunchtime and I am going to open a borrowed can of Campbell's soup, for Nina is not here to make me one of her excellent home brews. Peter is out to lunch.

I shall be adding a personal note to each of you later, but meanwhile I send my love to all of you.

Ever,

Nao.

⤙ ⤚

Moscow
28 October 1957

Dear Parents and Liz,
Dear Mother and Father Roberts and Mary,

It is quite strange; we thought we would not be able to call a single evening our own, on account of social commitments, yet behold, we neither of us got an invitation all last week, apart from a couple of do's "in the family," as it is called when Canadians entertain one another. This is splendid, and if it was not a freak week we can look forward to some quiet evenings at home and some less quiet ones at the theatre, at concerts, and at the ballet.

I will go back in my diary to the 16th, as that was the last time you heard from me at any length. On that evening we dined with an English bachelor called Ted Orchard and his three other guests — a tiny, informal, and most agreeable party, with some very good food as well as good company. Ted is one of the "Russian specialists" at the British Embassy and earns the title in every way. I am told that his political and economic knowledge is phenomenal, and his spoken Russian is much admired. There are a number of these specialists in the British corps, but I gather that Ted is the best. He looks like an academic and has a black beard. After dinner we drove home (in the chauffeur-driven Embassy car) one of the other guests, Ken

Scott, also British, and spent an hour listening to his records. That was the most pleasant evening we have spent in Moscow so far.

On the 18th I went to tea with Mrs McAlpine, wife of the senior British First Secretary. Then on Saturday the 19th we were invited to an American buffet dinner, at which the guests were required to wear a comic hat, and we nearly funked the party on this account (you know how Peter panics at the threat of having to put on fancy dress), but the hat business turned out to be fairly painless and the rest of the party was agreeably amusing. (Pa Z: Peter wore on his head the Greek shopping bag you brought me from your holiday, and it looked so dashing I think it will have to be reserved for similar occasions.)

Now we come to last week. On Monday we invited to dinner Bert, our accountant, and Carol, one of the stenos. As usual Nina was half an hour behind schedule and we had to skip coffee, as we were going on to the theatre, to see a famous group of Russian folk dancers. These were very good indeed. Some of their dances were quite thrilling, though in the second act they became a bit "Soviet," the worst being a dance in which all the children in the family come on a holiday to visit Mother on the Kolkhoz. There were at least twenty children, so she must have won the Star of Lenin several times over.

On Wednesday we had a good dinner with the Moores, together with our administrative officer, Frank, the newly arrived Naval Attaché and wife, Don and Ann Knox, and George Costakis and his wife. George is the Embassy's local administrator, who looks after us in relation to the local staff (and all other local domestic business). He is of Greek origin but has lived here for many years (possibly all his life?). His Russian wife is a Soviet citizen, though he I think is not.

George is a most interesting person who owns a fabled art collection, including several Chagall paintings; he knows Chagall personally. We hope to be invited to his home one day soon, after which we will tell you more.

Also on Wednesday our food order from Denmark arrived, much to Nina's and my joy. I spent most of Wednesday and Thursday unpacking the goods and arranging them methodically on the shelves in the storeroom in the Embassy basement. Then we at once started to prepare a new order for the things we had not thought of or had underestimated.

On Thursday we went to our first theatrical performance. The play was *Anna Karenina*, and as I am in the middle of reading the novel I was able to follow the scenes until the equivalent of page 490, after which it was all a mystery. I can't claim that I understood many of the speeches, but it was beautifully acted, and as long as I knew the story it was enough just to watch. Peter understood much that was spoken, but was exhausted after a couple of hours, and we left before the end, to the disgust of the coat-checking lady.

On Friday we tried Nina out on a bolder meal, when the Moores and the Knoxes came to lunch. We did not eat till nearly two o'clock, but it was good when it came. Considering that Nina has to cook on a stove that is big enough to hold one dish and one only, and that has no temperature control or even a thermometer, I think she does pretty well. This, our temporary kitchen, has two such stoves, but our own (future) kitchen has only one. Oh, and by the way, in answer to Mother Roberts's letter, there was far more wrong with our own kitchen than soap and elbow-grease could put right, but I have been promised some cupboards for it (now it has only open shelves), and the lavatory (toilet) tucked coyly beside the handbasin-cum-sink is going to be removed, and perhaps the tap can be repaired. As you have guessed, until recently it was a washroom, and was intended for the use of the Military next door (the attachés). The former kitchen for our apartment was down several flights of stone steps in the basement. The equipment was moved upstairs to our level in a moment of crisis when all the Houzers' servants threatened to quit if it weren't. But to counterbalance these inconveniences, we have a good big fridge, and a splendid freezer in the basement, very important in a country where supplies are unreliable, to say the least of it.

The bathroom is essentially not bad, but its hot water system is in too critical a state to be used at all, and the bath tap does not merely drip, it pours. It is rare to find a true craftsman in the Soviet Onion (as the clerks call it), and since a plumber is a craftsman it will be hard to get an adequate job of repair done. However, the admin. staff are definitely on my side, and I know things will be greatly improved before we move into our own apartment. Frankly, I don't know how the Houzers functioned as well as they did in these conditions, and I salute their spirit of endurance. Apart from the kitchen and bathroom, however, our new flat is very fine, and we will be happy there.

Later, same day. We've just had Vic Moore to lunch, together with Ken Scott, who was coming to see Peter on business. A minor crisis arose when Nina announced to me at a quarter to one (very red in the face) that the dessert had collapsed and I must think of another one, but quick. We saved the day on this occasion, but it had not occurred to me that she would produce no vegetables unless specifically told to do so, and we had a rather sparse main course as a result. Tomorrow Nina is being borrowed by the Turks for their national day, and I hope they manage better than we did on our ordinary weekday. The Turks did not invite us to come and be fed by our own cook.

This has been a strictly domestic letter, with none of my usual astute comments on Russian affairs, so you will just have to glean what information you can from the *Daily Telegraph* or the *Lethbridge Herald*. If you have any theory on the immediate future of Field Marshal Zhukov we would be glad to know it, though doubtless by the time you read this letter we will not be totally ignorant.

Much love to you all from us both,
Naomi.

Moscow
5 November 1957

My dear Ma, Pa and Liz,

I have not yet worked out how long a gap there is between the receiving and answering of letters — no, I mean the writing and the reading and the replying — though I know it takes a month for us to receive a reply to a question addressed to Lethbridge. Anyway, I think by now the parents must be home, and I hope they enjoyed the holiday.

Last week I sent by sea-bag a pre-Christmas parcel. As you know, we are limited in our monthly parcels to and fro, so I thought it would be a good idea to use our October allowance, since November and December sea-bags are likely to be much in use. This is what I sent: five highly decorative silver and gold dessert spoons "in the Russian manner." I believe they are made of real silver, but you will have to ask your jeweller. There are only five spoons because they were the only ones of that shape I could find, but if you like them I will keep looking for a sixth spoon. You may have to fetch the parcel from Canada House, and possibly there will be duty to pay; let me know if this is the case.

Now, in answer to your kind inquiries (unspoken but I know intended), I would like a 1958 diary for Christmas, and Peter would like a new typewriter ribbon for his Remington portable. However, we are still planning to buy a camera with our birthday money from Pa, so if we get just a jolly card at Christmas we will feel entirely satisfied.

But I do have a task for one of you, please. Would you be so kind as to arrange for the printing of 1,000 invitation cards similar to the model enclosed? And have them sent to us c/o Canada House? Please ask the shop to send the bill to us too. They should be on good quality paper.

No more now. Excuse the very domestic nature of this letter.
Much love to you all,
Nao.

— ~ —

Moscow
11 November 1957

Dear Parents and Liz,
Dear Mother and Father Roberts and Mary,

Now that the Anniversary is over maybe we shall enjoy a little respite from the propaganda. At the best of times there are more pictures in evidence of Lenin with his small eyes and his ruthless mouth than there were of Queen Elizabeth in Britain just before her Coronation, and in the past week this has been greatly intensified. Perhaps we are especially conscious of the Lenin pictures because there is so little advertising on display other than an occasional panel that tells us to "Drink tomato juice" or "Cross the road at the lights." Anyway, the last word in Lenin-ads appeared on Wednesday and successive nights: a dirigible (our old friend the barrage balloon) was launched into the sky and underneath swung an immense two-sided cut-out of Lenin, even bigger than the balloon itself, in full colour. This was floodlit from the ground, and as soon as it was dark all you could see in the sky was Lenin pretending to be God. Nikolai, our favourite driver, sighed and said it was "very beautiful," and we concurred dubiously.

Only Ambassadors and Military Attachés had tickets for the parade, but we were able to watch it on TV, and very alarming it was. At night we walked in the town, but apart from the crowds there was nothing special to see. There were some illuminations, so that normally dark Moscow for once looked like any western town on any weeknight, and some music was piped through loudspeakers, but no conspicuous gaiety was to be seen. Not that people looked miserable; they just milled quietly about, mostly in family groups, and once or twice we saw a group of young people start to dance, but the effort soon petered out.

Good news: our boxes of possessions from Ottawa arrived last week, as far as I know intact, though I haven't unpacked everything yet, for we are still in the Counsellor's house.

Work has finally started on our own apartment, but by the look of things it will be a long time before it is finished. The young women are filling up the cracks in the walls just now, ready to start painting. The method is to spread a layer of sawdust on the floor, cover up any lights or other objects left in the room, and then just slosh. There is no attempt to keep the paint on the item that requires painting, and they have a carefree experience that would be the envy of any schoolboy.

Later. It is now November 12th and we have just given our first formal lunch — only eight guests and ourselves, but it was a beginning. I ran up against all kinds of snares, finding myself yesterday at one point without food or extra servants, but it all came out all right in the end. I vow that in the future I will be completely self-sufficient in the food line, which shouldn't be hard, given our storeroom and our freezer.

Yesterday morning I tried to do a little local shopping for the lunch; I wanted frozen peas (which are sometimes available), heavy cream, and mineral water. I queued in two shops for about ten minutes in each, lost my place several times to people with sharper elbows and firmer voices, finally stated my requirements, but "*Nyet, nyet i nyet.*" Fine. So I went to the ice cream woman (whom I describe to Nina, when I want to distinguish the ice cream cart from the ice cream shop, as "the ice-creamly citizeness") and asked for some vanilla ice cream. Again "*Nyet.*" So I had to plan a new menu, especially as the chickens I had ordered via the office hadn't arrived at the shop — in fact they were delivered here the next day just as the last guest was leaving! I won't let myself be caught empty-handed next time (I hope). And I must say that once one has obtained the food the maids are wonderful at dealing with it and at laying a formal table. One can leave them pretty well to perform on their own once the plans are made.

We are going out to cocktails and to a dinner tonight, and several more times this week. I am half sorry, as it is nice to be home at night, but also half glad, as we began last week to think that no one was ever going to invite us again.

Mother R. asked what we wore at these functions. Cocktails, lunches, teas, and informal dinners are easy. A black suit will get you by on all these occasions (plus perhaps a hat at a cocktail party) and a black dress is perfect, in fact any smart dress such as one would wear to a similar do at home. But I find black-tie (i.e., formal) dinners quite puzzling; very few women wear full-length evening dress (to my dismay, as I have three), and the so-called short evening dress I don't consider evening dress at all, but rather a super cocktail dress. (Even the one you helped me buy in London, Liz, is really too dressy.) I am going to attend a few more formal dinners before I make up my mind what I need, even if I am incorrectly dressed for the time being, then I can supplement my formal wardrobe when we go on leave. When I unpacked my long-lost clothes last week it didn't seem possible that I should need anything else, and I am not anxious to start shopping again.

All for now. Much love,

Nao.

❧

Moscow

26 November 1957

My dear Family,

Peter has written to his parents this week and you are just getting a scrappy letter from me.

Thank you, Ma and Liz, for letters and for commissions performed. I can't tell you how useful it is to have agents in London. I want to open up a sterling account, and will do so, but meanwhile, if you don't mind, I'll just write you dollar cheques to be deposited in your own banks.

Here comes another request. I did not mean to bother you with this one, but Harrods are proving so hopeless that I am afraid I must. I ordered from Harrods various things for Nina, but they have ignored two important items, and I wonder if you would mind coping?

What is needed is footwear, and the important thing is to be able to return the shoes if they don't fit. Do you suppose that our nice Mr Turner in the village would oblige? I have promised Nina a pair of winter boots like mine, calf length, zip-fastened, wool lined, good quality but not so expensive as to cripple me financially (appropriate verb ...). I think mine cost about three pounds three years ago, so they would cost about four pounds now, I imagine. The other thing we need is a pair of black shoes suitable for waiting at table, slip-on style, sturdy rather than elegant, not too high a heel but not flat either. Suede or leather, to cost two to three pounds please. Size is of course the problem. She thinks she takes a size 6 American, i.e., a size 4 British, but I am sure she cramps her foot and it should be a size 5, and rather broad at that. So would you be a dear, Ma, and send me off a pair of boots and a pair of shoes, both on approval and capable of being exchanged, if necessary? I am sure you are a more reliable shopper than anyone on Harrods staff.

Yes, I received my Harvey Nicholl's catalogue, thanks. Lots of lovely useless things, but fun to look at when you are in a country with no jolly window displays.

Sorry, Liz, but as I don't read the Russian press I can't tell you what is being said about Sputnik, but I gather there is a certain amount of boasting. Our servants say that they are pleased that Russia achieved it first, and when is America going to produce one? But I don't think they are particularly interested in it qua sputnik.

No, we won't be taking any leave at Christmas, though we may be able to get away in February or so, after our new Counsellor has arrived, and we will be just ripe for a holiday then. We would probably take only a few days, just to have a change of scene.

Liz does not mention in her last letter the possibility of working in Ghana for a year, and we wonder if the plan has fallen through. Hope so, as we (selfishly) want her to be in Europe while we are.

We are dickering with a returning American for a super camera to be paid for with the birthday money Pa gave us. I'll tell you more if we purchase it.

It is possible that Chris (or Kris) Moore, the wife of Peter's colleague, will be coming to London for a few days in early December to buy maternity clothes, and she may get in touch with you. I think you would find her invigorating company and she is very pretty.

Peter is in bed today with all the signs of a bad cold. We don't tell his family when he is mildly sick, as they tend to become alarmed at the thought, and it seems a waste of emotion if he is already better by the time they read the letter.

Much love to you all,
Nao

———

Moscow
28 November 1957

My dear Parents and Liz,

I don't know whether Naomi wrote to you about Kris Moore, who will post this letter when she reaches London. She is the wife (since six months) of our second secretary Vic Moore, and we and he will be grateful if you will invite her to the house before she returns here on Dec. 6. She is staying at the Mayfair Hotel.

Just so you know, Kris is a beautiful and very nice Swede, divorced some years ago from a Frenchman by whom she has a son John, age about 5. He is in Moscow. She is shortly to have another baby, a Moore this time of course. The Loridans (Belgian Ambassador and wife), who have been so kind to us, are her particular friends. If you have time and feel equal to it, I can vouch for Kris as someone you would enjoy.

I shall write separately by the next bag to tell you about the wonderful 35-mm camera that Pa bought Na and me for our birthdays. Meanwhile thanks to Ma for invitation cards. Please don't give a thought to the short space supplied for the date information. In Moscow all invitations are by telephone, and cards are used only *pour mémoire*.

Love to you all,

Peter

———

Moscow
1 December 1957
(My Ma's birthday)

My dear Parents,

Thank you, Pa, for a very handsome camera birthday present to us both. It's a Nikon, Japanese imitation of the Leica, 35-mm, and said to have a better lens than the Leica. I have this from a Canadian physicist now in Moscow, who, before he bought his own camera, looked at all the lenses available, and found Nikon to be second-best, Leica third-best. I've forgotten what came first. I bought it from the departing assistant American Air Attaché, having first looked at and admired a lot of pictures taken with it. So far, the weather having been dull, I have taken only a few pictures around the embassy (including the cop at the gate, who didn't like it one bit) and a few in Red Square yesterday while Na was doing some shopping in GUM. I have a black and white roll in now, but as soon as I know how to use the camera properly I shall take nothing but colour slides.

The invitation cards are in use, for a men's lunch that I am giving on Thursday. Please don't fret about the date space, Ma. I notice that many other cards don't have more room for the date than ours do. Nobody in Moscow sends cards, anyway, until they have first invited you by phone and know that you are coming. It's a curious way of going on. Incidentally, I notice that Belgian third-person cards instead of having R.S.V.P. have R.S.L.P. printed at the bottom. I think that's carrying grammar too far.

My men's lunch is my first venture in this field, but my experience so far has been that this is much the most useful kind of entertaining. The talk is all shop, and often pretty good. I'm having the American first secretary, a man from the British secretariat (as they call it — it does research on internal affairs in the U.S.S.R.), our own Ambassador, the Italian second secretary, and the *N.Y. Times* correspondent, Max Frankel.

We stayed out last night to the unwonted hour of 4:00 a.m. at a "charity" in the American Embassy, to raise money for the Anglo-American school. It was quite good fun, with every Western and neutral diplomat in Moscow present; there was drinking, dancing, and an amateur floor show, which really wasn't very good. The Americans did best with an imitation of Harry Belafonte, the British were in doubtful taste and not very funny with a Salvation Army turn. Then the Americans balanced things with a really dreadful men's chorus, and the British redeemed themselves a bit with a performance of Swan Lake's *pas de quatre* by the Air Attaché and others. It really wasn't worth staying out so late for, and I don't know why we did it. But I noticed the American Ambassador dancing cheek to cheek with somebody at 3:30 a.m. Of course it was his house.

Next week is just pleasantly full. We have a dinner at the British dacha, where two couples, poor things, live permanently, 17 km. out. I have a lunch with the Foreign Ministry (they do this from time to time) and we have a dinner to meet a Russian from one of the institutes who seems to have attached himself to the Embassy. Then we are giving a lunch for some of our own staff on Tuesday, as well as the lunch I'm giving for the men. That leaves us a few evenings for ourselves for theatres or for reading, of which we are both doing quite a lot. I'm going through Yeats complete and chronologically for the first time. Great stuff. I'm also reading some Canadian poetry but so far haven't found any poet I want to read again except P.K. Page, a woman.

When Pa comes here, is he thinking of asking Khrushchev for an interview? Everyone else does.

Is Liz going to Ghana, or not? Would you give her my love, please, and tell her to forget about the flask, but thanks for trying. I won't need it until I start travelling in the country.

Sorry this letter is so addled. I've just finished two other long ones, and I've wearied the muse — which was a bit jaded anyway because of last night's party.

Much love to you both, and to Liz,

Peter

━ ⌣ ━

Moscow
2 December 1957

Dear Ma, Pa and Liz,

Dear Mother and Father Roberts and Mary,

It won't be long before we get into our own apartment. It has been repainted and a little man is busy scraping the floors with a razor blade. The kitchen is vastly improved, and though not a convenient shape one can work in it. I consider the stove its most inadequate feature (now that the lav. has gone), and I can't think why, considering that we import fridges and deep freezes and vacuum cleaners, we don't also import stoves. I had thought that ours was so primitive just because it was old, but I've discovered that the new ones now on the market are exactly the same. A new snag I have just noticed is that we have no means of broiling anything; the heat (gas) comes only from below. Not that all this affects me particularly, but I am full of admiration for Nina for coping as she does. It will be nice to get settled, but at the same time I shall be really sorry to leave this place, which is very cosy and much more spacious.

We had an interesting experience last week. We tried to get into a vacant taxi but were obliged to yield to another customer, and a young man, seeing this, tapped Peter on the shoulder and said "Come with me." He then piled us into his car, which was parked just down the road. Once we were inside, we realized of course that it wasn't a taxi at all. The young man was indulging in a spot of private enterprise, and he simply asked us to pay him what we wanted at the end of the journey. It wasn't until we reached home that he realized that we lived in an Embassy building, and then he was very upset, because the Militiaman would see him. So we let him drive us half a block past the Embassy and then pull up, but I don't doubt that he was spotted anyway and will have a hard job explaining why he had foreigners in his car. Poor chap. I forget if I have explained that not only Embassies but any building in which foreigners live is guarded night and day, to make sure that no unauthorized Soviet citizen gets in, and if one is identified trying to do so he is questioned closely as to his business. The formula is: "Aren't you making a mistake, Citizen?" and if we can contrive to look like Russians (but we can't) we will be challenged in the same way when visiting other Embassies or foreigners' blocks.

We do have the odd casual contact with Russians in the street and the shops and at shows, but one cannot follow up an encounter by arrangement without exposing the Russian to some risk. Of course there is the other kind of contact, which has been cleared beforehand with the police, but this is not of much interest to us and is of rather too much interest to "Them."

Last night we visited the famous puppet theatre, the Teatr Kukol. It is quite brilliant and extremely funny, both comic and sophisticated. The show we saw is called *The Unusual Concert*, and represents an amateur performance given in the provinces, complete with massed choir, gypsy dancers, tango dancers, a conjuror, a lion tamer, a performing dog and a singing chicken, a baby-prodigy pianist, a baritone who sang German Lieder, and an American-style male quartet together with a slinky, husky female soloist, whom the announcer characterized as having "sexappeala."

We offer this show as a strong inducement to anyone who considers visiting us here, and we can promise at least one thoroughly enjoyable evening.

We did buy the high-quality second-hand camera, and are now bustling through our first roll of film, anxious to see how the camera performs. Peter is thrilled to bits with it, and dashes out in his lunch hour to take pictures of the back door.

Speaking of pictures, last week we were invited to dinner with the Pakistani Third Secretary, who, after dinner, showed us on a screen photographic slides he had made. This is a form of entertainment I disapprove of in principle but welcome in practice, as viewing provides a welcome rest from trying to make conversation. Also, his pictures were very good.

The only other party last week was the big charity ball at Spasso House in aid of the Anglo-American School. (Spasso is the residence of the American Ambassador and is simply magnificent.) There were all sorts of sideshows and raffles, and a cabaret that we had heard talked about ever since we arrived in Moscow, but that (we thought) was not all that good. The ball was preceded by dinner at our Ambassador's for all the Canadian staff who were going to the event. Very good of Mr Johnson, don't you think?

I intended to do some cooking today for a lunch we are giving tomorrow, and I sent Nina off early in order to have the kitchen to myself. But now the kitchen is full of plasteresses, and also we have been requested to come and fill a gap at our Ambassador's table tonight, so I don't know when I am going to prepare the dishes I had planned. At least we are both invited to grace the dinner table on this occasion. Sometimes the Ambassador needs an extra woman only; in this case (if I am the one appointed to this role) Peter is invited to join the guests before dinner and to re-join them for coffee and brandy, etc. after dinner, but is served his meal with the kitchen staff behind the scenes! He would prefer to do without dinner and be allowed to stay home, but on the other hand he says that he gets a good opportunity to practise his Russian in conversation with Marousia (the cook).

I will now add a personal note to each family. This is the end of the collective letter.

Personal part for the Zimans:

Thanks so much, Ma, for looking after the invitation card situation. The cards you ordered are perfectly splendid, and there is nothing to worry about at all. Thanks for being so quick to respond. Thanks too to Liz for taking so much trouble about P's flask. He had the idea of going round making friends with the locals by pouring them drinks from his little flask, but I think he has decided now to do nothing until he starts going on trips, probably in the Spring. I asked him if he thought he was a St. Bernard dog.

Thanks also to Pa for enabling us to buy the camera. I doubt that we would have done so if he hadn't encouraged us.

I understand that the leg of our parcel allocation coming from London (as opposed to Ottawa) is not limited, so if you have managed to get Nina's boots please do send them right away, as she keeps inquiring about them.

In reply to Pa: There isn't a Dutch Ambassador here just now, but we know the Chargé quite well. We've met their no. 2 man too, though not so often. All the Belgians are agreeable. We especially like Depasse, the no. 3 man, who has an ulcer and can't eat away from home, and who has a very nice wife.

It is all right, Ma, it was on the day *before* our lunch that I went on my frustrating shopping expedition, not on the day itself.

Again, love to you all,

Ever,

Nao.

◦— ～ ◦

Moscow
9 December 1957

My dear Parents and Liz,

What good agents you are! Thank you, Liz, for dealing with the atlas, and thank you, Ma, for taking care of Ant Mud's hamper. (I think Peter asked you to organize a hamper for Cousin Judy, too, didn't he? And sent you a cheque?)

Ma, you were quite brilliant over the boots and shoes. Nina hops around for joy in her new boots, which are *very* handsome, and even if they had not fitted her I think she would never have allowed me to send them back, but would rather have cut off her toes like one of the Ugly Sisters. The foot part was in fact perfect, though they were a bit tight at the zipper part where it turns the corner, so to speak, but we think this will yield in time. The serving-at-table shoes were a stroke of genius: very soft and slipper-like (and she makes a great fuss about wearing only soft shoes) and yet quite smart. She is particularly pleased with the heel, which is exactly the height that she wanted. I must say her whole appearance is changed when she has on a decent pair of shoes. It was noble of Mr Turner to let me have them on tick, and I was happy to be able to impress Peter, who thought this could happen only in Lethbridge.

You realize that as a result of being so efficient you have let yourselves in for all kinds of chores? Feeble Harrods *still* have not sent their parcel, after more than two months. Thanks for sending another batch of invitation cards, and also Aunt Leslie's Christmas present, which I have hidden from us.

Speaking of presents, I am sending with this letter two tiny packets (one each) for Ma and Liz, which please don't open till Christmas Day, as I would like to imagine you opening them at that time. I haven't found anything for Pa, but may have done so by the time the bag goes. Anyway, he should know that any parcel that arrives for him is intended for Christmas, and the same rules apply.

I hear that Kris spent an evening with you but have not seen her since she got back yesterday, so don't have any details yet.

Yes, I will write a circular letter to the relations sometime. I find as I did when I first went to Canada that I have to keep repeating myself, which I hate doing, but it is no good expecting new readers to start at Chapter IX. I do mostly keep carbon copies of the letters that I type (though not of course of the hand-written ones), so I may be able to crib from some of my own letters to the two families. But if I write anything confidential I dare not keep a copy here, so your file will be more complete than mine. This answers your query about the diary I asked for; it was meant only for noting engagements, not for recording "great thoughts" and critical comments, which should not be left lying around.

The Ambassador, Vic, and Peter had lunch last week with the Deputy Under-Secretary and a couple of relevant officers from the Foreign Ministry. Peter says the talk was pretty vitriolic, though they managed a few toasts. Peter was impressed with our Ambassador for talking straight and frank to them, with no concession to bourgeois politeness. The meeting took place in one of the splendid houses that the various Ministries maintain for entertaining, and the meal was Russian-style and quite good.

On Thursday I went to a huge tea party given by Adrianna Turpin, British wife of a fairly senior American diplomat and also a friend of John Ziman's wife, which is probably the reason for my invitation. I was the only non-American guest there, and even at that the other thirty to forty guests did not account for the full quota of American wives in Moscow. At our own Embassy, apart from the wives of two military attachés, only Kris and I wave the flag for Canada, which is pretty silly, as she has never been there and I am still a newcomer. At the beginning of February the Counsellor and wife are expected, and as far as I know she is a native-born Canadian.

We gave two lunches last week, one just for four of our own staff, the other a Men's Lunch for the Ambassador and four others, each of a different nationality. I cooked the meal for the first lunch, and got Nina to copy it for the second lunch. So that is one more menu to add to the Embassy's rather limited repertoire. Peter's guests stayed until four o'clock, so I guess it was a success. (It is permissible to leave a lunch at three o'clock.)

On Saturday we went to a buffet dinner and dance at the British dacha, which is 17 km. outside town and yet is lived in all year round by two Embassy couples. I rather enjoyed the country-cottage atmosphere (a bit like an Austrian country home, with inside galleries hanging over the main room).

I bought Peter a Russian fountain pen the other day that is an exact copy of a Waterman. And for Christmas one of my presents for him is an electric razor, which looks identical to the picture of a Phillip's Phili-Shave that I saw in a magazine. The only difference is that the Phili-Shave costs about $25.00 and the Russian model about $8.00. I can hardly wait to see how it works. I suppose world patents are not valid in Russia, which must be very convenient. I notice that the vacuum cleaners in the shops are of similar design to the new Hoover Constellation, a globe with a long nozzle attached.

Our own flat is all but ready, which is just as well, for hordes of workers are now over here doing their re-decorating, and I have already retreated almost to the bathroom to escape the falling plaster.

I'll stop now, though I may add a word if I see Kris before Wednesday.

Much love,

Nao.

P.S. Kris just came in, fresh with news from home, which made me feel very homesick. Many of the foreign wives go off on trips to western Europe at small provocation, and there is nothing to stop me doing the same, except that since it is Peter who works and I who idle I feel it is he who needs the holiday and not I. So I will wait at least until we have been away together once before I talk of sloping off on my own, much though I long to see you all.

Thank you so much for inviting Kris. She obviously enjoyed the visit and appreciated being fetched by Pa. I wanted to question her closely about everything, but restrained myself. She said, "So far as I could tell, they were all in good form," which I thought was a most sensible comment. People so often make assertions about the well-being of comparative strangers when they have no means of knowing what is the normal state of the person discussed. I'll be interested to hear your comments on the evening.

Thank you, Ma, for the Christmas pudding charms. I have at least four tinned puddings and will try to sneak the charms into one of them, and perhaps retrieve some for a later feast. I will have to make sure that I share one of the charm-laden puddings with Harry, who is the oldest of the Embassy clerks, i.e., security guards. He once lived in Edmonton, London, but emigrated to Canada as a boy with his mother. Even after so many years he seems still typically English.

Much love, again,

N.

Moscow
18 December 1957

My dear Parents and Liz,

Here it is, bag-departure day for the Christmas mail, and I haven't time to write a proper letter. All the end of last week I spent moving us to our new apartment (which I think we are going to like very much) and today we are giving a housewarming eggnog party for all the Canadians who belong to the Embassy, which will need a certain amount of preparation.

Last week there were some interesting events and engagements, but these deserve a proper description, so I won't attempt to write of them today. In fact I must stop at once and look up some eggnog recipes. There will be a much better letter next week, I promise.

So, here's wishing you all a happy Christmas. Oh, and there is a parcel for Pa in the bag today (Liz's and Ma's last week) and an envelope, all to be opened on December 25.

Much love,

N.

Moscow
20 December 1957

My dear Lethbridge and London families,

I hear that the bag is to leave on Monday this week, as Wednesday is Christmas Day. So I have got time to bring you up to date on last week's activities before embarking upon next week's.

Last Thursday we took Lilya (who is my English pupil, Peter's Russian teacher, and George Costakis's daughter) to a Soviet play that had been recommended to her, and it was most interesting, so much so that Peter was able to write a long dispatch about it. The play is *Sonnet of Petrarch* and its message is that it is only the old orthodox Communists who see everything in black and white; the new Communists realize that there are many shades of good and bad, and that it is possible for a man to permit himself certain indiscretions in his personal life without necessarily being politically unsound. The minor roles of the two stupid, unimaginative old-line orthodox Party officials were exceptionally well played, and the audience roared with laughter at them. I understood very little of what was spoken but was nevertheless able to follow the story, which is an indication of how good the acting was. It certainly isn't a first-rate play, but it came as a surprise to us that jokes about orthodox Communism would be permitted. Not, of course, that there was any suggestion of criticism of the current regime, only of earlier unimaginative interpretations of Party orthodoxy.

It was quite warm when we went into the theatre, but while we were inside the temperature must have dropped ten degrees, and it was the coldest night yet when we came out. There was not a taxi to be found (usually one soon picks one up) so we walked Lilya to her home — all of us moaning with cold — and she tried to phone for a taxi from there. No taxis at the ranks, so Lilya went outside again and cleverly found us a private-enterprise car owner, who drove us home, or rather who dropped us off near to the Embassy but out of sight of the guard at the gate.

The next night we were again at a theatre, but this time we were at the Bolshoi, as guests of the Foreign Ministry. The occasion was the appearance of guest-artist Beryl Grey, no. 2 dancer at Sadlers Wells. (Oh, no, this was on Sunday, not Friday, for she had to cancel Friday's performance on account of illness, and there had been time for only one rehearsal before Sunday's show. Imagine having to get up and dance when one is suffering from Moscow tummy!) The ballet was *Swan Lake*, and a perceptible gasp rippled through the audience when Beryl Grey made her appearance in the second act. For a dancer, she is enormous! I think she was just the same height as her partner, but she has extremely long feet and was most of the time on pointes, so she usually towered over him and dwarfed all the other members of the corps. One could see that the Prince was distinctly worried when he had to lift her over his head, and he looked alarmed and surprised too when her long foot whizzed past his ear in the high kicks. Nevertheless, from what we have been able to glean, the Bolshoi troupe loved her and thought very highly of her dancing. The audience was most enthusiastic (but then they always are in Moscow), and she returned for curtain call after curtain call. After the audience had begun to wend its way out one could hear the company applauding their guest behind the curtain. Those who know said that her technique was superb, and without being a good judge of technique I know that her dancing was quite lovely to watch. I was so relieved to find that there was an English dancer up to Bolshoi standards, and we all felt sneakily delighted that the Muscovites would know that there was at least one Englishwoman who was not "decadent." If anyone sees in the press a review or comment concerning B.G.'s Russian tour, I would like to be told where to find it, please.

To go back a day, on Saturday we were at a very pleasant and informal dinner party given by British colleagues, Derek and Lileke Thomas. (Lileke is Dutch, but so excellent is her English that before I knew this I had taken her for British born and bred.) They are delightful hosts, and as all our fellow-guests were either British or American we were able to enjoy a relaxed not too international evening, which went on until 3:00 a.m. and ended with Derek playing the piano and the rest of us joining in intermittently in song.

On Monday this week Peter and I, together with the Moores, were invited to dinner at the Costakis home, probably the only Russian home that we will ever get into, and scarcely typical at that, for George has a large and (by now) extremely valuable art collection. It includes about a dozen Chagall canvases, a Bracque, a Picasso, and many works by some significant Russian painters of the early years of the twentieth century (the avant-garde artists) whose names I am afraid were unknown to me. He also has a tiny room where in a crowded display on the walls are many splendid icons of all ages, some of which would be the pride of a museum collection. But apart from his pictures, George's home surroundings appear to be normal, that is, rather cramped quarters in an old and shabby building set in a quite pretty courtyard, and the use of a kitchen shared with several other families. (But they do have a two-and-a half-room flat for a family of five, which I gather is unusually generous.)

At the end of last week and the beginning of this week I was busy moving us into our own apartment, and on Wednesday we gave a housewarming party (eggnog) for all the Canadian staff, from the Ambassador to the guards. It was a bit of a fiasco, and we told the Moores, who arrived long after the other guests had left, that they were lucky to have missed the party.

Our apartment is very nice, if a trifle chilly. I will leave a space at the end of this letter and will try to draw it. Most of the furniture is pretty shabby but may be renewed one day, and anyway we don't mind much so long as it is comfortable, which it is. Our spare bedroom is also a music room, where Peter has his piano, guitar, and recorders, and these give him immense pleasure.

Nina is tickled pink to be back here, works hard, and is usually good-humoured. Having established the fact that I am not going to try to keep her overtime night after night, she is now reluctant to go home even when I beg her to leave, and starts doing my laundry or cleaning silver or some such non-urgent task at eight o'clock at night. She is a true "charac-ter," very independent in all her views, and given to cracking some quite comic jokes. In short, we like her. Mind you, when she so chooses she can be thoroughly disagreeable, but she has not been so toward me lately, and anyway she never seems to bear any resentment after a tiff; rather an endearing and child-like trait, don't you think?

This brings you up to date and almost to the end of the year. My next letter will comment on the contents, as yet unknown, of the many parcels that have been rolling in during the past few days. Thank you all in antic-ipation.

Happy 1958 to everybody.

Much love,

Nao.

P.S. The attached sketch will give you an idea of the layout of the apart-ment. You will notice that access to the spare bedroom is through either the main bedroom or the dining room, and that resident guests must pass through one of these rooms in order to reach the bathroom. This degree of intimacy may put off some potential guests, but not family, I hope.

Moscow

26 December 1957

My dear Liz,

Very many thanks for the handsome and useful pair of leather gloves. I am delighted to have them, for until now I had nothing between fur-lined and fabric gloves. Yours nicely fill the gap.

Yesterday (Christmas Day) we attended a lay Matins at the American Ambassador's residence (the Anglo-American church meets alternately there and at the British Ambassador's residence), then came home and had a private present-opening ceremony, before going upstairs to join all the other Canadian staff for a 2:00 p.m. dinner at our own Ambas-sador's. We enjoyed a good Christmas meal followed by presents for all the

Russian servants and token gifties for the Canadians that Santa (Peter, of course) found under the tree. The Ambassador also gave little extra presents to the four wives (Kris and me and the two military wives). Very nice of him, wasn't it?

Nina was not asked to serve at the Ambassador's dinner, and whether for that reason or for some other reason, she was (and is) in a truly foul mood, and merely grunted when I gave her present to her, and the parcel is still lying unopened on the kitchen table.

After the Ambassador's party we drove with Vic to the Costakis's home, where George is ill in bed. We ought not to have called without warning them, for we got a good glimpse of how they really live, and it must have been embarrassing for them. George's bed is in the tiny living room, and there he lay looking like death, with his wife, three children, and an unidentified man all carrying on their various occupations around him. We appeared all unexpectedly, armed with expensive presents for them, and felt uncomfortably like Lady Bountiful visiting the Poor.

At ten o'clock we sallied out again, this time to a Commonwealth Ball given by the British Ambassador and his wife. Sir Patrick (Reilly) is a great party spirit, and thanks chiefly to him the whole thing went with a bang. In addition to ballroom dancing there were musical games, Scots reels, country dances, Sir Roger de Coverley dances, and other jolly British institutions. People mixed very pleasantly: cooks, guards, first secretaries, stenos, and counsellors all pranced around merrily together. We stayed until 2:00 a.m., which is quite unlike us at such functions.

Alas, today is an ordinary working day for the Canadians, and all last night's merrymakers are sitting at their desks looking jaded.

A very happy 1958 to you, in the course of which we expect to welcome you to Moscow.

Thanks again for the gloves.

Ever,

Nao.

———

Moscow
28 December 1957

My dear Parents and Liz,

You did send us a lot of nice and carefully chosen prezzies to help out our Communist Christmas, and we are grateful. I loved the Ziman triptych (both of us did, of course), which now adorns the top of my piano in the music room (which will become the guest room when any of you come to see us). Lizzie's typewriter ribbon and handkerchiefs are practical and welcome contributions (neither of them obtainable here). So thank you all very much indeed.

Pa's offer of books and periodicals is very kind. At the Embassy we get all the English periodicals I have time to read — *Encounter, Statesman, Spectator, Economist, Manchester Guardian Weekly,* and so forth — so there would not be much point in sending these. But books, yes, please; we would be grateful for almost anything Pa would care to send along. Speaking of sending things, I think there is likely before long to be trouble about the bag service from London to here and the reverse. The Queen's Messenger has been complaining about the enormous burden that he has to pack in and out of the Canadian Embassy every week. (Members of the British Embassy are more restricted in what they may send in the bag.)

It is indeed exciting to hear that there is some prospect of a visit from the parent Zimans (though no word of Liz in this connection). I shall discuss with the Ambassador the problem Pa raises and will let you know by the next bag. It would be much better, obviously, if you could be free to write when you get home, and if you had some help with your fares from the *Daily Telegraph.* I wonder if the direct London-Moscow flight will be in effect when you come. Unlikely, I think. The quickest way now is Paris-Prague-Moscow, but a more interesting way, I should think, is Copenhagen, Stockholm, Helsinki. It takes all day by that route, however.

Na will certainly want to tell you about the Christmas party with Sir Patrick and the one with our own Posol (Russian term for Ambassador), and all the other excitements that went on and still go on.

And now, much love to you all, do keep writing, and we will see you before long. By the way, there was the first mention the other day of my possible official ten-day visit to England next summer. But nothing definite yet. Of course we would combine it with some leave.

Much love and
S novim godom!
Peter

———

Moscow
31 December 1957

My dear Parents,

Your friends the Robertis are coming to dinner here on January 8th. I met Paola at a party the other day, and it is lucky that I did. I had issued my invitation in person to her husband, whose understanding of English is not as good as one thinks. I had asked Vero if Paola's son would still be in Moscow on the 8th, and he said "Of course." I asked, would the son like to come to dinner too? "Of course." Then to make quite sure, I repeated, twice more, that we would expect the three of them, him and his wife and his wife's son, and he agreed enthusiastically. Then, at the party, I learned from Paola that not only would the son not be there on the 8th, but in fact he had never come to Moscow. I didn't let on to her what had happened.

Glad to hear that Pa attended a dinner at which George Kennan was present. Last night I finished *Russia Leaves the War*, which I have been reading off and on for three months. I read it very carefully and it has taken me a long time, but I was not bored at any time. He does write well.

On Mary's birthday, 28 December, we telephoned her and the parents-in-law in Lethbridge and had a splendid connection. The service was really efficient and pleasant, which is not what one expects in the Soviet Union, and all the more impressive for that. We had a six-minute talk for about twelve dollars, hardly more than the Ottawa to Lethbridge rate. It was 7:30 at night here and 9:30 in the morning in Lethbridge.

How nice of Ma to take all that trouble to administer the gift of two hampers for Peter's relatives. I'm sure they will be appreciated. Thank you too for explaining the currency routine to me. Obviously I need a sterling account and I am going to ask Pa to take the enclosed dollar cheque to his bank and re-open my account there. But this time it will be a dollar-deposit account such as Peter had in Oxford; cheques can be written on it in sterling but only dollars can be deposited in it. Would you do that, please, Pa?

You have been such faithful and obliging London agents during the past months.

Now I must stop and do something about something.

Much love,

Nao.

—◦~◦—

Moscow

7 January 1958

(Orthodox Russians' Christmas Day)

Dear Everybody,

I have been writing separate letters lately to each family, so some of this will no doubt repeat what some of you have heard already, but perhaps you will excuse that.

The bag has been thrown all out of schedule, but so far as I know we are back now on the regular run for letters — namely, they leave here on Wednesday night. But for the time being the Ambassador has stated that we will send no parcels until some new arrangements can be made. As you know, the Queen's Messenger takes all our stuff as far as London, from where it is forwarded as necessary, and though the British are allowed to send nothing private other than letters, we Canadians have been allowed to send a private parcel each month, up to five pounds in weight — in fact, as it seemed that nobody checked the weight we had developed the habit of sending anything and as much as we wanted as far as London. I don't know whether the Q.M. was under the impression that the Canadian parcels he carried were all official ones, but anyway, when just before Christmas he found his diplomatic bag saying "Mama" every time he shifted it, he decided it was time to point out that he wasn't Santa Claus. Several little girls who are now the proud possessors of Russian dolls should be told that they unwittingly caused what might be known as a diplomatic incident. The local mail is probably safe enough, but if my information is correct, parcels going abroad have to be packed in wooden crates. I am hoping that soon we will have made a new arrangement regarding parcels.

New Year passed very quietly for us. The servants had a holiday, starting on Tuesday afternoon, which I regard as a holiday for me too. The night of the 31st we spent at American friends, the Turpins, together with two other couples, watching a private showing of *War and Peace*. Considering all things, it was remarkably good, and at least had the effect of making those who hadn't read the book want to start reading it at once (I am one of those people). We had finished watching the film by midnight, at which point we ate mince pies and toasted the New Year, and went home about one o'clock.

Peter and I walked home, and certainly there was more sound than usual coming from the apartments, singing and talking and gramophone music, but the streets were as quiet and orderly as ever. I gather that New Year, though their most important holiday, is a time for staying home and enjoying the company of friends and family — without the western compulsion to go out and be noisy in public. All the shops and public places are decorated in the same style as ours are for Christmas, with fir trees and strings of coloured electric lights and glass bobbles and Santa Claus, only here he is Uncle Frost and wears a white coat, not a red one, and has a daughter (I think) called Shnurrigan (I think) who mollifies him when he is in a bad temper. Among my own tree ornaments made of glass are some little figures who look very like the Three Wise Men, but cannot be.

Wednesday was a holiday and we did nothing special. On Thursday we went to a play, *Odna*, which wasn't bad, and made up for a rather dreary story with the usual excellent acting. On Friday Peter and Lilya went to another play, but P. found this one beyond him and understood almost nothing. Also on Friday we gave a small lunch party for the visiting Anglican priest and five other guests, which turned out to be a surprisingly merry and successful affair. I wish there were a guarantee that all our parties were going to be as painless.

On Saturday Lilya, Peter, and I went skating in Gorki Park. I was sent to the beginners' rink (where there are parallel bars one can hold onto) and several little girls helped me when I got into difficulties. (Really, the children here are remarkably nice.) My situation was made far harder for me than it should have been, for the pair of skates I had rented had a nail sticking up into the left boot on the inside, and when I removed the boot I found that the nail had bored a hole in the sole of my foot. No wonder it hurt. I sloshed iodine liberally on the wound, and haven't yet developed lockjaw or blood poisoning. Russian boots are short, so that no ankle support is provided. I'm thinking of writing to Stockholm for a pair of my own.

On Saturday evening we had dinner with a journalist friend and his wife, Max Frankel of the *New York Times* and Tobi Frankel. They live in one of the hotels and had just moved from their one-room accommodation to a two-room suite, and were delighted with their new quarters. An evening in the hotel made me appreciate our apartment more than ever.

Yesterday, Monday, the weather suddenly became bitterly cold, after having been quite mild for some weeks. Today I see that it has snowed, so maybe it will not feel quite so cold. I didn't go out at all yesterday except by car to dinner with two of our stenographers, where we had a pleasant evening. We were very envious of them for having a mild, gentle, good-tempered maid, who actually *likes* them. When Nina springs her foulest moods on me I often think of applying for another maid, but then I hear about the laziness and inefficiency of the maids assigned to most other foreigners, and I feel I would be mad to part with Nina, for she has neither of the above faults. She is also honest, and *when* she is nice she is very nice. The girls were lucky enough to get a maid second-hand from the British, but most newly hired maids and cooks have to be trained from scratch, something I would not do well. So I expect that Nina and I will jog along as we are; thank heavens, we are in calm waters this week, after a very turbulent Christmas and New Year's season.

I recently got in on a preview presentation of a film about Russia made by Associated Re-Diffusion for British ITV, called *U.S.S.R. — Now*. I quite enjoyed it while I was watching, but thinking it over afterwards I decided that it had been rather bland and highly idealized. There were too many interviews of this sort: "Ah, so you want to be a cameraman when you grow up. Tell me now, what made you first think of becoming a cameraman?" The film was made on an exchange basis: the British cameraman was given permission to go "anywhere" (I question this) and was given all kinds of help, in exchange for ditto for a Russian cameraman in Britain. The conditions for the exchange were that the film was not to be political, and erring, I suppose, on the right side, the British-made film made Russia look the next best thing to heaven. I would love to see the Russian-made film, in order to check whether they were as conscientious in adhering to the terms of the agreement. Anyway, if you should get the chance to see it in Britain, or if it is sold to a Canadian network, don't miss it, for there is certainly lots worth seeing in it, despite my general criticism.

I don't think there is any more news to report from this end, and we didn't receive letters from Canada in the last bag, so there is nothing to answer in that direction. I will answer the London letters on a separate sheet.

So that's all for now. Much love from us both,

Nao.

Moscow
10 January 1958

Dear Macalister Family,

At last I am starting on the promised report of my reactions to the Soviet Union (or Soviet Onion, as our clerks call it). I am a little hesitant to write this sort of letter, as my feelings about Moscow tend to change radically from day to day, and if I re-read this letter tomorrow I may feel that it is a thoroughly inaccurate account. However, here goes with a description of the way it all strikes me *today*.

To start with our own rather secluded life: Peter and I live in a pleasant two-bedroom flat right in the Embassy, which is the former home of a rich sugar-merchant of pre-Revolutionary days. It is a two-storey building, of which the upper floor is the Ambassador's suite and the ground floor is all offices, except for one corner, which is our apartment. In the basement there is a mass of storerooms, most of which I have never been into, but one of these is equipped with shelves where we may store our imported foodstuffs (canned goods, bottled goods, dry foods such as cereals, etc.). Behind the main building is a little garden, the garages, and the Counsellor's house, reserved for the Counsellor and his family, with the exception of part of the upper floor, which is home to the three Security guards. Those of the staff who don't live on the premises — that is, the other Secretary, two Administrative Officers, four girl stenographers, three service attachés and their clerks — all live in foreigners' apartment blocks in the suburbs. (Foreigners are not permitted to live in buildings occupied by Soviet citizens.)

All our servants and drivers are Russian ("local staff"), provided by *Burobin*, the agency that looks after the domestic concerns of foreign residents, and may not be by-passed. We have no close contact with any Soviet citizen apart from these employees and a specially chosen few (chosen by the Soviet authorities, that is), and we do not normally follow up on any casual contact we make, for fear of incriminating either the Russian or ourselves, so I am afraid that my comments and observations will perforce be superficial.

My own daily life is rather idle. I have an efficient if temperamental cook-maid whom I inherited from my predecessor so mercifully did not have to train, and my time is therefore mostly my own. I am ashamed to say that I have not done anything very profitable with it in the four months we have been here. I spend a ridiculous amount of time reading cookbooks and searching for recipes that can be adapted to fit our conditions.

The social life is fairly active. We find that we go out to dinner or lunch about two or three times a week, and give a dinner party ourselves about twice a month. These events are part of the job, of course, though they may also be enjoyable (however, often not, I am sorry to say). For the officers the parties are a continuation of the working day, their purpose being to let colleagues exchange views and share the crumbs of information they have obtained from live Soviet sources or from a close reading of the newspapers (including photographs of public figures and their placement in relation to the Leaders) and of public documents. These gleanings contribute to the dispatches that the officers prepare for their Departments at home.

The dinner parties are to my mind unnecessarily elaborate occasions, particularly given the challenge of obtaining good quality fresh produce. Not that I am complaining about the need to attend so many of these functions, for if we, the wives, were not invited we would lead very isolated lives. We can at least contribute to the discussions the nuggets of information or opinions that we have picked up while shopping at the market or sightseeing. I expect the officers, too, may even welcome the opportunity to meet in a social setting and to develop friendships, just as in the real world outside the diplomatic bubble.

In the Canadian mission (and I suppose in most others) we receive a generous "representation" allowance, which enables us to entertain often and in style, so there is little excuse for shirking that duty, and the Embassy maids and cooks on call for formal functions perform admirably well. (We borrow extra domestic staff from one another as needed.) All the same, one does enjoy an evening at home without company.

(Averin, who has long experience as a Foreign Office wife, will probably tell me that what I have just described is a situation familiar to all diplomatic families abroad.)

We do, fortunately, have some evenings when we are free to attend theatre, ballet, or opera performances. The only one of the last that we have been to was disappointing, but the ballet of course is superb, and the theatrical performances, though I understand very little of what is spoken, are nevertheless well worth attending, for the acting is so vigorous and so passionate that I can nearly always make out what is going on in spite of the language difficulty. Most of the theatres I have been in are very pretty (though the seats are uncomfortable); they look Victorian, with an abundance of red velvet curtains, tassels, fringes, and glass chandeliers. As a matter of fact this is true of public buildings in general; one sees the same decoration in the shops and hotels, and even in people's homes on the rare occasion that one can get a glimpse through the window-curtains. "Home" as far as we can tell, usually means one room with a table and as many beds as can be squeezed in. There would likely be a common washroom and kitchen for several apartments. The housing problem must be the most acute of those the government is trying to deal with in the domestic realm, though I understand that outside Moscow matters are not so bad, in fact many families who live in one room in Moscow actually own a dacha (summer cottage) in the country, where they are able to spread themselves a bit on holidays.

The two things that struck me first about Moscow were, first, the breadth of the streets and the handsomeness of many of the older buildings (formerly private homes, now mostly offices), and second, the crowds. I still gasp sometimes when I go into the more central part of the town; the crowds are so thick, all day long, that people automatically fall into two columns, those walking up the street and those walking down the street, and it is impossible to do other than to follow the pace of the crowd, always a very slow one. In the shops it is the same thing: a swarming mass of people or else an orderly, patient queue. They don't seem to mind this at all, in fact I have the impression that many people queue just in order to see what other people are buying, rather than because they are looking for something for themselves. The shortage of goods seems to be more acute than the shortage of money, for wherever there is something to buy there are people to buy it, even apparently useless things like ornaments and glass dessert bowls. But it is not only for goods that they queue; yesterday I saw an enormous lineup for the new art exhibition, and on any day one can observe a queue in which individuals may stand for as long as four hours before reaching their objective, namely the opportunity to gaze at the embalmed bodies of Lenin and Stalin, known to disrespectful foreigners as "the gruesome twosome."

Like the other members of the Canadian staff we import a lot of canned and packaged goods from an export firm in Copenhagen, but apart from these supplementary foodstuffs we live on the local economy, which is pretty good on the whole. Supplies are a bit unreliable, and fruit and vegetables are very seasonal (oranges, mandarins, and apples, beets, turnips, potatoes, and carrots are the choice in the winter), but that which one can obtain is all good. The actual shopping is a very tiresome procedure, and I lazily leave it nearly all to my maid. I do go with her, though, to the open-air market where the collective farmers come in to sell the surplus products from their private plots, and though things here are more expensive than in the shops, it is worth the extra roubles to feel that one is supporting the only form of private enterprise. (Shops don't have names: they are Second-hand Shop no. 24, Canned Goods Shop no. 102, etc.)

Now to people. As I said, the only Russians we get to know at all well are our servants, each of whom is a very distinct personality. They are generally willing and friendly, especially the Embassy drivers, and we soon become attached to them. The strangers one bumps into (often literally) in the street tend to be rough-mannered but not unfriendly. They are intensely curious about foreigners, whom they instantly recognize as such, and they stare at us relentlessly, sometimes fingering our clothes to see what the material feels like. In the shops, if I betray an interest in buying something, all other custom ceases, and shoppers and saleswomen are completely preoccupied with me and my purchases, interpreting my Russian between them and offering advice, or else just staring and using their elbows to get a bit closer to the source of the excitement.

The Russians appear wonderfully kind to their children, and one rarely hears a child crying. Toys and children's books are excellent and imaginative by any standard. The public parks and gardens are set up with little slides, and in the winter even the tiniest children, as soon as they can walk, are likely to acquire a pair of skis or skates. The children are rather silent and docile, with very round, very pink faces, and seem to be perpetually good-humoured. In winter the babies are wrapped closely in blankets, papoose-fashion, which are then bound round with satin ribbons, so that they are unable to move anything but the tips of their noses. The walking-size babies are so thickly muffled in fur coats and scarves, also fur bonnets, that their arms stick out at right angles to their bodies.

The weather in winter is depressing, for the sun rarely shines and the sky is an overall gloomy grey (quite unlike sunny though equally chilly Ottawa). There is a snowfall nearly every day just now, but the streets are kept clear thanks to the efforts of an army of women workers (many of them quite old) equipped with shovels and spades and brooms. After the women have done their stuff, special snow-clearing trucks not unlike the Canadian version come along and pick up the piles of snow.

Some things in the Soviet Union are very efficient, like the Metro, which is swift and clean, with stations of great architectural and decorative magnificence. Other things are primitive, like my oven, which has no temperature control, or like the little man who scraped the floors of our flat when it was being redecorated by means of a razor blade; he later sanded them by shuffling around the floors on a piece of sandpaper.

So far we have not been outside Moscow except for a brief glimpse of Leningrad, where we changed from the boat to the train, and much of what I have described in this letter may very well not apply outside this city. But I have offered you a few random impressions, and perhaps when we have been here longer and have travelled a little in the country I shall be able to write with more authority. Also, of course, when my language skills have improved and I don't have to qualify every quotation with the rider, "at least I think that's what he said."

Each week we like it more here. Our life is comfortable, quiet, and generally peaceful, and the Westerners whom we meet at diplomatic functions seem an exceptionally nice bunch. So we've no complaints.

With greetings to you all from us both,

Ever,

Naomi.

Moscow
13 January 1958

My dear Parents,

The missing parcel has turned up! I am delighted with both gifts; they are really lovely. It is a pity that the nightie is a nightie, as it is much too pretty to be confined to the bedroom, but I shall enjoy wearing it just the same. Not till the summer, however, for this is a rather cold flat, the bedroom in particular being almost as cold as an English bedroom. Luckily I brought with me a couple of all-enveloping flannel nightgowns, and these are what I wear here during the winter.

The artificial flowers are fantastic. Everyone who comes in says, "I didn't know you could find carnations in Moscow just now," or else, "Does Peter fly you in flowers from Germany?" In other words, they look convincingly real. And are they in fact real, only preserved in wax? (I wish someone had thought of doing that to me five or six years ago.) I've put the flowers in the George III pewter mug and they improve the living room no end. So thank you both for two excellent, well-chosen presents.

Now the request of the week. Could you or Liz order me a pair of skates, please? Size seven and a half, please, in order to leave room for a stout sock. I should have asked you ages ago, but thought we might be taking leave in February and I would be able to buy my own skates then. Now it looks as if we won't be thinking of leave until April.

By the way, John Ure of the *Baltika* and the British Embassy tells me he used to work for Benn's Publishers and often heard Pa's name mentioned by Mr (Glanville?) Benn.

Much love,
N.

Moscow
14 January 1958

Dear All,

One twenty-fourth of 1958 gone already. Fancy that.

It has been very snowy here recently, but not unpleasantly cold. I am very bad in that I will stick indoors for days at a time unless I have a real reason to go out, for the sun shines only about fifteen minutes per week, and there is something very uninviting about a perpetually grey sky. The snow is of a quite different quality from our snow in Ottawa, for it does not stick on branches or roofs but always falls to the ground. There it is quickly cleared away by women with shovels and men with special trucks, which have scooping hands at the back. The snow clearance is really very efficient, much better than it was in Ottawa, where traffic might be held up for half a day after a heavy snowfall. At first one tends to be rather shocked to see the women out in their skirts and aprons shovelling and sweeping, especially as most of them appear to be in their sixties or older, but I am beginning to think that they quite enjoy the activity (except perhaps in the worst weather), for they keep warm by virtue of the exercise and chat to one another as they work. Nina tells me that they work only five hours a day and earn five hundred roubles a month and they don't pay rent for their room — at least, that is what I understood her to say, but I may have got it all wrong.

Our dinner party last Wednesday was a big success, which I suppose will make us feel all the more acutely the failures to come. All the guests were good value, but especially Mrs Roberti, the wife of an Italian correspondent here who has been a friend for many years of the Ziman family. Mrs R. is really very amusing in a mad, inconsequential way.

But it was another guest who was the sensation of the evening. He is an American economist, and has been trying ever since he came to Moscow six months ago to get an interview with the editor of an economic journal that he considers the least untruthful Soviet publication in existence. The interview was finally granted for six o'clock Wednesday evening, after which he was to come on to us at 8:30. At about 9:30 his wife begged us not to wait any longer for him, and we sat down to eat (incidentally the best meal, except for the Belgian one, that I have eaten in Moscow: borscht, creamed crab, roast grouse, crepes Suzette). I think it was about 10:15 when the economist finally roared in, hardly able to stand and feeling terrible. Our collective jaws dropped, until his wife gave voice to the general verdict by exclaiming in extreme surprise: "Why, he's drunk!" I gather that he normally is very abstemious, but during this interview he had nobly tried to keep up vodka for vodka (indeed, it is impossible to refuse on these occasions — all agree on this) for three solid hours. The remaining forty-five minutes had been spent in the editor's car, together with the other two members of the paper's staff who had been present at the interview (or party), while they drove up and down our street looking for the front door, which none of them was in a condition to recognize. Unlike most drunks he was really very likeable, and took our teasing in good part, in spite of feeling so ghastly. He wasn't able to eat a thing, and finally fell asleep in his chair, from which he was gently removed at midnight and promptly tried to climb out of the window, after saying fervently to me, "Thanks so much, and I do apologize, old boy."

He rang up next day to beg forgiveness, which wasn't at all necessary, as one felt it had not been his fault at all. Anyway, he was the first one to arrive in the office that morning, and was delighted with his interview, which he hopes will lead to other things, so altogether it was an exciting evening for us all.

The following evening we were at a fairly big buffet dinner and dance, which was a standard affair, neither good nor bad. Peter and I agree that a dining-room meal is to be preferred to a buffet occasion, even if it means giving two parties instead of one.

On Friday night we went to another play, in yet another delightful little theatre, and this time with padded seats, which none of the others has offered. It was Tolstoy's *Power of Darkness*, a very sombre play about peasants, and therefore even harder than usual to understand — the peasant speech, I mean. But it was superbly done, and we were completely carried away throughout all four hours of the performance. The sets were extremely convincing, and the acting of a fervour that I have rarely seen in the West; they throw themselves into the part with such intensity that upon occasion you can clearly see the tears rolling down their cheeks. The acting in the other plays we have seen has been good too, but I think there is more scope in this pre-Revolutionary drama than in the Soviet plays, which have to conform to such arbitrary specifications. This one was performed by the Maly Theatre Company, like all the others a repertory company; I understand that it is the most famous theatre, with a long-established tradition, and it more than lived up to the reports we had heard.

On Saturday we were at another buffet dinner, this time a smaller affair (eleven people altogether) and somewhat boring so far as I was concerned, though Peter had quite an interesting talk with the men. (In Moscow, exchange of views among the Westerners being almost the only basis for dispatches, the men tend to drift together at parties in order to talk shop, which practice is rather hard on the women.)

On Sunday we did nothing, and on Monday went down to the British Club and saw a fairly amusing movie called *Le lit*. We walked there and back (about twenty-five minutes each way) by a very pleasant snowy night. The British have a wonderful view across the river to the Kremlin, and I always like passing that way, especially at night and in the snow, when Moscow looks its romantic best — no, "romantic" is too soft a word, for it is strong and secret and exotic, and one senses the past very strongly when walking across Red Square. (This sounds like a translation from a foreign tongue, but blame that on Moscow.)

By the way, I have been meaning to say to Mother Roberts, in answer to her request to us not to get into strange people's cars, that she need have no fears for our safety. The Moscow people are extremely law-abiding, the Militia (police) are everywhere, and no Soviet citizen would dare to assault a foreigner. At night the streets are not empty; even after midnight people are out walking (perhaps taking a break from their crowded apartments), and of course the street-sweepers are at work. In fact I feel much more secure outdoors at night here than I did in Ottawa. Also, we are completely safe in our own homes, since we have our Militia-man to guard us. Admittedly, he is not there for our protection, but he keeps out the strangers we *don't* want to see as well as those others, so it works both ways. As it is, we leave money and valuables lying around and never bother to lock doors. Private papers, of course, are a different matter, and these have to be locked in the safe or incinerated.

That's enough for this week.

Much love to one and all,

Naomi.

P.S. to the Zimans: Peter is looking into the question of Pa's writing for publication after your visit. He has to write to Ottawa for approval, and it doesn't sound promising.

— ᵔ —

Moscow
15 January 1958

Dear Pa,

I am going to write you a proper letter to be sent in the next bag; this is just to say that I have consulted Mr Johnson on the problem that you raised in your letter of December 22. He said that obviously it would be best from our point of view if you did *not* intend to write upon your return, but that he did not wish to discourage you from doing so. He suggested that I seek the advice of the desk officer in Ottawa, which I am doing by this bag. I will let you know as soon as I have a reply.

Incidentally, you might be interested to know that *Pravda* of June 6 informed its readers that "malice is exuded by the *Daily Telegraph* and the *Daily Mail*, newspapers of those British political circles that bear a high responsibility for the ruins of Port Said, and the destroyed villages of Oman and Yemen, for the deaths of thousands of people in Kenya." I haven't the slightest idea what effect this might have on your chances for a journalist's visa. I should not think much, since the *Daily Express*, presumably equally guilty, has had a couple of men here recently.

Love to Ma and Liz, as well as you,

Peter.

⌒〜⌒

Moscow
20 January 1958

My dear Parents and Liz,

I misled you somewhat concerning our bag privileges; it is just the Moscow-London bag that for the moment is restricted to letters only, not the incoming bag. (And you thought that was the end of your shopping commissions! No such luck.)

We are inviting the Robertis (third time for him, second time for her) to a party next month to meet our new Counsellor. We are glad to have them as guests, as everyone is delighted to meet journalists, as a change from diplomats, and though we meet the same American correspondents at many of the parties we go to, we seldom meet the Robertis outside our own home.

Thank you for all the newspaper cuttings, especially (Liz) the one about Beryl Grey, which I have pinned up in the outer office. And thank you, Liz, for your letter. It's remarkable how regular the family has become in its letter-writing, quite unprecedented since schooldays. I think you are almost as bag-conscious as we are.

No, we could not purchase for you an air ticket paid for in *our* roubles, for the Canadian government subsidizes them in order to permit us to live in "representative" style in Moscow, and they would hardly consider the paying of visitors' fares "diplomatic representation." Either you or we could, however, exchange currency at the tourist rate (40 roubles = one pound, 10 roubles = one dollar) and buy a ticket for a Russian plane trip part of the way, or all of the way if the service has extended that far by the summer.

Glad your friendship with the two Hungarians is flourishing. Do they both work in the Library? No, on second thoughts, don't write to me about them, especially don't mention names, as they may have relatives still in Hungary, and we have to be very careful about such things.

Poor Peter has sprained his wrist playing — guess what? — charades!

Lots of love to the three of you,

Nao.

⌒〜⌒

Moscow
28 January 1958

Dear Everybody,

Happy wedding anniversary to both sets of parents!

Some changes have occurred since I last wrote. For the past week I've been taking someone's place at the kindergarten of the Anglo-American School and will continue until she comes back next Thursday. There is one other kindergarten teacher, the wife of a British officer, equally unqualified, and about twenty-six children of various nationalities. All are from diplomatic families and most of them speak some English, though there are three or four who, I suspect, don't understand more than one sentence in a hundred of what we say to them.

School is from 9:15 to 12:30, which leaves me with my afternoons still free. I really rather enjoy the work, if you can call it that; the children are delightful, and particularly interesting for being so foreign. I find myself especially charmed by the non-Western ones, Pakistanis, Japanese, Indonesians, Indians, and two very impish Ethiopians. Unfortunately, my first Moscow employment coincided with my first Moscow cold; also it is a fairly heavy week socially, so I am feeling a bit jaded, but I think it is mostly the cold that is responsible. It is nice to get away from Nina in the mornings — I never see her till lunchtime these days.

I laughed at your comments (both families), after you had viewed my sketch of the apartment, that Nina had a long trudge from the kitchen to the dining room, and so would she have done if I had told her. To get to the old kitchen, before the move to the Military's washroom took place, she had to go down the main Embassy corridor, up five stone steps, down twenty-four more stone steps past the back door of the Embassy, and along a flagstone corridor in the basement. How our predecessors ever got anything hot to eat I can only guess. Now our kitchen is considerably nearer to our dining room than the Ambassador's kitchen is to *his* dining room. Notwithstanding the difficult temperament of some of the maids, I don't know in what country one would ever find better servants who are willing to work in such challenging conditions. When it comes to preparing party food and setting a fine table and serving the food at table, they are marvellous, and they seem to enjoy the parties, too.

On January 25th we gave a dinner for twelve in celebration of Vic's fortieth birthday. I had Nina ice on the birthday cake in Cyrillic script "Vic — 40 lyet" (*sorok lyet*), because those were the words that appeared on all the banners, etc., at the time of the Fortieth Anniversary in November. Once again we had a late guest, this time a journalist waiting for Khrushchev to finish a speech. We did not wait for the guest this time, but he had to be given a meal when he came, at about 10:30, and so the maids were late getting away again, which is awkward for me. Normally Moscow guests are very punctual.

A cocktail party last night was unusually interesting. It was India's National Day of Independence, and the Boys were there in full force. The Indian Ambassador and Bulganin made one another flattering and fulsome speeches, and Khrushchev, Mikoyan, and all the others whom I don't recognize applauded and swigged lemonade, which is all that the Indians are allowed to provide on their National Day. The party was held in the Sovietskaya, a pre-Revolutionary hotel, very gorgeous. On this occasion the Boys had strong competition for the attention of the journalists, photographers, and other guests, for among those guests were Elizabeth Taylor and her husband Michael Todd, visiting Moscow for I am not sure what reason. (Their American hosts must have asked for an invitation to the party for the pair.) I was very close to E. Taylor a couple of times; she is tiny and has remarkably beautiful eyes. Mike Todd is also small, and is rather dried-up in appearance. He is reputed to be churlish, but he was quite genial yesterday. They were both at the American Club last Sunday, where some of our clerks talked to them. Fun to be in Moscow when Hollywood comes visiting.

Other parties since I last wrote to you include a dinner at the apartment of some nice Finnish people, and another at the American First Secretary's. There was a dance at the British Club one Saturday and a skating party the following Monday. After supper at this party we played charades, in the course of which Peter sprained his wrist! (We know how he dreads party games, but this seems an extreme response.) The British doctor bound it up for him on Tuesday, and he now has the bandage off and thinks it is about better. I guess it wasn't a very serious sprain, though I think it ached a bit the first days.

What else? Did I tell you, or did Peter, that he is now a Second Secretary? This makes some difference to his salary, but more to his prestige.

A story I've been meaning to tell you: remember our famous Chinese horse, sent to us as a wedding present from Hong Kong? When we left Ottawa we decided to leave it in storage, as it would be irreplaceable if damaged. Well, a couple of weeks ago, what should I see in a shop of books and paintings from the People's Republic but our dear old horse, all got up in Chinese fashion with a roller top and bottom instead of a frame. We bought the whole thing complete for a quarter the cost of framing our Ottawa horse, which we had supposed was an original. The new horse now hangs in splendour in our dining room. We felt that the joke was on us.

No more now. Much love to you all and thank you for your letters (and, Pa, for setting up my bank account).

Ever,

Nao.

━━ ～ ━━

Moscow

2 February 1958

My dear Parents,

There's really no point in writing you a letter now, because Nao will be in England in exactly a month, and I soon after that. It is now likely that I shall drive from here to Brussels with the American first secretary David Mark, who is by long odds the best value in Moscow now. He's a first generation American; his Pa was a Lithuanian Jew.

We'll leave March 2 (subject to getting a visa) and take five days to go Minsk, Brest, Warsaw, Prague, Frankfurt, Brussels. Nao will, I think, leave March 1, by air, arriving same day in London. The business I'm on is that which I mentioned to you in September, and lasts two weeks. At least five days of this is out of London, and life will be irregular in other ways, so I am proposing to take a hotel room for myself (on the government, of course). Nao will presumably be *chez vous* if you have room. I believe the evenings when I am not out of London are free, but I am anxious to keep the one weekend (March 15–16) for seeing the relatives I missed last time. We'll probably leave London on March 22 or 23.

We are extraordinarily busy here, what with Bulganin letters, massive changes in internal affairs (agriculture), and old Khrushchev shooting off his face about the religious hypocrisy of Mr Dulles. Not to mention the Canadian election coming up, and the possible withdrawal of Canada from the ranks of the neutralists, which is what they now call us here.

Na has a cold this weekend and had to be left at home while I went round the Kremlin in clear, cold weather, taking colour photos of all the golden towers and other splendours of that place. It's almost the only ancient monument in Moscow, though there are many pleasant pre-revolutionary buildings and some Soviet horrors that are at least interesting.

We saw on TV a week ago the Soviet documentary film of Britain. (The two countries had a swap, and censored one another.) It was eminently fair and even generous, though there was some emphasis on Marx's grave,

G.B. Shaw, etc. Even a few introductory remarks by old man Rothstein. No sign of the Red Dean. I enclose a transcript of an *Izvestia* article about the British film made in the Soviet Union.

Now enough. See you in five weeks.

Love to the lot

Peter.

FILM ABOUT SOVIET UNION OVER BRITISH TELEVISION

V. Matveyev, *Izvestia* London correspondent

Millions of people in Britain saw in the evening of January 28 the full-length film *The Soviet Union Today* televised by Associated Re-Diffusion. This film was specially made for the British television by a group of British and Soviet cameramen, headed by Michael Ingrams, representative of Associated Re-Diffusion, who spent several weeks in the U.S.S.R.

At the same time a Soviet group with the help of British colleagues made a film about life in the British Isles. (This film was shown over the Moscow television also in the evening of January 28. –*Ed*.)

A good beginning was made for further co-operation of Soviet and British cultural workers in such an important sphere as television. Why then did this auspicious undertaking arouse the malicious hissing of some British circles? The showing of the film hardly ended when the floor was given to a *Daily Telegraph and Morning Post* "critic" who tried to accuse Michael Ingrams of making a "propaganda film." This "critic" obviously acted on the principle of wishing to see only spots on the Sun, and not light.

Well, all the worse for this "gentleman" and others like him.

(*Izvestia*. In full) THE END

Moscow

3 February 1958

Dear Pa:

In spite of the harassments of Bulganin, our desk officer in Ottawa got off a quick reply to the letter I wrote him a fortnight ago, and the following is the relevant paragraph from it:

"Since your father-in-law is a professional journalist, we think that he should not be barred from carrying out his professional activities in the Soviet Union merely because he is related to you and wishes to make use of your hospitality while he is in Moscow. We suggest that you advise him to come as planned but to emphasize to the Soviet Embassy in London when he applies for a visa his intention of doing a series of articles for his newspaper. Similarly, when he is in Moscow, we suggest that he gather his information in a somewhat independent way and that he make a point of seeking help from Intourist and other agencies to impress upon them the fact that he is carrying out his work on his own as a professional journalist. Thus, for example, if he wished to visit a factory or a place of historical importance, it would be well for him to apply on his own as a journalist, rather than to have the arrangements made by yourself or someone in the Embassy. I am sure he will understand also the desirability of avoiding in his articles any reference to yourself or the Canadian Embassy."

Thank you for your offer of stuff from the *Sunday Times*. Yes, please. We get the *Observer*, but no other Sunday paper.

Love to you all,

Peter.

❦ ❧

Moscow

3 February 1958

Dear Parents and Liz,

Isn't it nice that business takes us where we want to be? I guess I will arrive in London about March 1, and will sleep at home if there is room. When Peter comes I can continue with you or else stay at his hotel, whichever seems the more convenient. If there is no room at home, I can go straight into a hotel or lodgings, if you will please book a room for me.

I love my kindergarten teaching, and am sad to have to stay away today in order to give my cold, which is now a cough, an extra day to clear up. Next Thursday the teacher I am replacing comes back, so my job comes to an end. I completely lost my voice on Friday, and had the doctor look at me on Saturday and prescribe me some medicine. I spent the weekend in bed and am up but indoors today. No temperature but lots of coughing and snuffling. On the whole, though, we've been very healthy since we've been here.

Thanks for the Beryl Grey articles in the *Sunday Times*, a paper we don't get, though we do get the *Observer*. I found them very interesting. Our Ambassador met her at a dinner while she was in Moscow.

I haven't done any work on my Russian for weeks, and I become less and less articulate. Really, I must settle down and do some work on it. You would be ashamed of me.

What a pity that Peter says that I may not come on the car trip through Poland and Czechoslovakia. Of course I would love to, and the driver (David Mark) is willing. But Peter thinks it may be pretty rugged. At least it will give me an extra week in London while I wait for the travellers to arrive.

If all goes well, see you soon.

Much love,

N.

⌁ ⌁

Moscow
10 February 1958

My dear Ma, Pa and Liz,

The latest plan is that I should leave here on February 28 on the once-a-week jet, the famous TU–104, to Copenhagen. From there I fly BEA Copenhagen to London, flight BE–221, arriving 17.45.

If you should think of meeting me, do check with the airport regularly, as the Aeroflot planes seem to be more often off schedule than on. The Crowes, who were supposed to arrive last Tuesday, had to wait until Friday, and then were packed onto a very slow plane instead of the jet. We expected them at 8:00 p.m., then at 3:00 a.m., and they finally arrived at 6:00 a.m. It was quite a night for Peter, who was meeting them. They seem to be a very nice family. With several small children, they must have found the journey a strain.

The skating boots arrived safely and are very beautiful. Now I am going to see if I can find Russian blades to fit them.

See you soon.

Love,

Nao

⌁ ⌁

Moscow
12 February 1958

Dear Everybody,

To take up this week's story where Peter left off (in his letter to Lethbridge and Winnipeg):

We gave our dinner for the Crowes on Monday, and it went not badly, much better anyway than the last dreary affair we gave in this house. There was good food and lots of chatter (though very little wine drunk, I was surprised to notice when totting up the losses), and the guests stayed much longer than courtesy required, the last one not leaving till 1:15.

Although the party was officially in honour of the Crowes, I had arranged the guest list and the menu with half an eye to the Ambassador, since I had never entertained him before (though he has been to a men's lunch here). I thought I had assembled a good cross-section of people he did not know and was feeling quite smug, and then on Sunday night he developed a fever and therefore could not come on Monday. I managed to fill his place at the last minute, but now I still have the problem of entertaining Posol for the first time.

The Crowes seem delightful people, and keen on getting about in Moscow, and I think they will stir us up a bit against the lethargy that has affected us during the last few weeks. Also I think that when spring comes I shall be more daring at using my mornings for exploring — I don't find the cold weather conducive to outdoor activity.

Last night we went to see and hear *Boris Gudenov*. I was rather disappointed. The visual part was fine, spectacular sets and costumes and a crowd on the huge Bolshoi stage of more than a hundred performers at some points, but we all thought the singing strangely lifeless, with the exception of one old man who sang a single melancholy song in heart-rending tones. But four and a half hours was a long time to sit to hear one song and admire eight sets. (Part of the time spent inside any theatre is devoted to the very lengthy intervals, during which all the spectators march slowly around in a clockwise direction, while they examine one another's shoes. It is a tradition that drives us foreigners crazy, especially as it is our shoes that receive the most attention.)

To Mary: oh, but we don't overeat. As a matter of fact my too tight dresses seem to have become loose again. Peter has perhaps put on a little weight, but in fact he needed to do so.

Love to you all,
Naomi

Moscow
17 February 1958

My dear Parents,

Thank you for all your letters — "all" because we got in the last bag some that were presumably intended for the bag before.

Our social life has become alarmingly brisk, in fact we have a straight run of a dinner party every weekday night from Wednesday until I leave Moscow, plus a cocktail party before dinner on several nights. (I must have told you already that it is simply "not done" to refuse an invitation unless one has already accepted a previous invitation for the time and date, and diplomats' Moscow is too small a society to permit one to break this rule and hide out at home or elsewhere.)

Now that Mrs Crowe has arrived, I am starting on my "calls" in the morning. I am too junior to go un-presented, and although Kris is of a level that she may present herself, she is too junior to present me, so I have been lucky up to now, and was forced to wait until a more senior wife joined our group. Then the lucky ladies who receive us will have to return the call, probably the following week. If you are wondering what we will talk about on these occasions, you are not alone. (I don't know whether this practice extends to foreign missions where the diplomatic corps melds with the general population; I expect I will find out in time.)

The skating boots arrived (oh, I already told you that), and I bought some Russian blades and had them screwed on by a *spetsialist*. The work is so crude that I hate to think what damage a non-specialist would have done. However, they are quite fit for the purpose and I was able to try them out on Saturday when we were invited for lunch and skating at a dacha where a couple from the British Embassy live. It was great fun, and thanks to the new boots I was able to glide around quite skilfully — well, I fell down only once in a couple of hours. The ice surface was quite good, but the air was very mild, a wonderful combination.

No more now. I expect you will see me before you get my next letter. If I have any general news I will send a carbon of whatever I write to the Roberts family and we will all be able to read it together on Tuesday morning.

Looking forward to seeing you, and thank you for all your welcoming noises,

Love,

Nao.

* * *

Moscow
31 March 1958

My dear Parents and Liz,

Just to show how times change, we started off our second session in Moscow by going to two cocktail parties this evening, one at our old friends the Germans, the other at our old friends the Japanese. Butter wouldn't melt in any of their mouths.

The trip was pleasant but for the descent at Moscow, which gave hell to Naomi's ears again. A Soviet airplane looks like a badly worn corner of an

Edwardian middle-class drawing room, lugubriously transplanted (the interior, I mean). But it seemed to get there all right. Nina had been at work, and had the flat shining and spotless, food in the refrigerator, etc. All very nice and much above our station. Still winter here, although very little snow in the city.

You were wonderfully kind to us the last three weeks, and it has made a really big difference to our attitude to life here. We're both ready to take on the Russians again. I especially enjoyed the lunch and the dinner with Pa at the Reform Club; a good memory to bring back to the back of beyond.

Na will doubtless be writing too. This is only to thank you from me. Love to you all,

Peter.

———

Moscow
1 April 1958

My dear Parents,

Many thanks for a lovely holiday. It was horrid to have to leave, but once we were back things looked much brighter than I had expected, especially as the sun now shines all day, and we got a big welcome from all our Embassy colleagues. I will tell you about the journey in my next letter, so that the Roberts family can hear about it at the same time. There won't be time for me to write a decent letter before the bag leaves tomorrow.

Peter seems to have left his hairbrush behind! Did you find it? If not, it may have fallen out of the camel bag, which entirely lost its zip fastening between London and Copenhagen. Well, we'll buy a Moscow one, and perhaps if the two missing ones are ever returned he could open a travelling exhibition of Hairbrushes from the World's Capitals.

What a fright I got when I found we were overdrawn on our dollar-deposit English bank account. I discovered it ten minutes before the airport coach was due to leave, and with Peter, white-faced, shouting "Criminal offence" at me, I just had time to phone you. Luckily, on the coach I was able to find my Canadian cheque book, and at the airport managed to obtain paper, envelope, and stamp. We had five minutes in which to write a letter and sign a cheque to be paid into our sterling account, and I gave the precious burden to an air hostess to mail, which I pray she did right away. It would take the bank a few days to claim the funds from Ottawa, but at least they will have our cheque by the time people start trying to cash the cheques that we wrote on Saturday or Sunday. By the way, seven kilos of excess baggage cost us six pounds, four shillings!

All for now. Much love and thanks,
Ever,
Nao.

———

Moscow
9 April 1958

Dear Everybody,

I have only just heard that there is a bag leaving today, so this will not be the long letter you were all hoping for. From now on, I believe, the bag will be leaving every Monday, not Wednesday as formerly. This week things are odd because of Easter.

We had a wonderful holiday and feel so much better for it. I didn't realize how the strain was accumulating until we got outside the Curtain, when suddenly all one's troubles slipped away and the world looked quite a tolerable place. Not that life here is at all bad, but everyone agrees that it is important to get out, even if only for a few days, every six months if possible, if one is not to become irritable and scratchy.

We have both come back rosy-cheeked and full of energy, and I am proud to announce that thanks to my time spent whizzing around London I have lost one inch in each of the vital places (today's statistics: 34, 26, 36) and all my previously skin-tight dresses look like fashionable sacks. Now we are busy planning various trips within the Soviet Union, which should be fun. Meanwhile, I am committed to six weeks in the kindergarten, starting next Monday.

The journey back was quite pleasant and uneventful. It gave us a splendid opportunity to survey the differences between appearance requirements for service personnel in the West and in the East, which differences were well characterized by our various air hostesses. The BEA girls were tall, slim, and impeccably dressed, and the Finnair girls were shorter but equally slim, and very blond and pretty; the one and only hostess for the entire plane on Aeroflot was a little dumpy woman with greasy hair and a bad perm, who wore a mud-brown raincoat, lisle stockings plus ankle socks, and emitted strong wafts of the familiar Soviet perfume. Nevertheless, she was very pleasant and industrious; she had to prepare all our suppers by hand (none of this pre-packaged nonsense), and she spoke quite good English. She was also touchingly concerned when my ears started playing up in their usual way as we descended; we weren't flying very high, but the cabins are not pressurized. This time, the pain wore off within a couple of hours of our landing, so it wasn't too bad.

One of our drivers was at the airport to meet us, and he gave us such a big welcome that suddenly it was nice to be back. As always, our passports were seized from us before we were allowed out of the plane, and it was half an hour before they were returned to us. During this interval we watched the treatment given to an American couple who had been on the plane with us. So far as we could gather, they had come as tourists, and he could speak a little Russian, from which we guessed that perhaps he had been Russian-born, or maybe his parents had been Russian. Anyway, no Intourist man had turned up to meet them, and they weren't getting much help from the airport officials. On the contrary, when we left, after offering our services if needed, the customs man was going methodically through every piece of luggage, and all the porters and miscellaneous workers were crowded round and peering at the poor woman's packed garments as the official inspected each separate layer in each separate case. (Incidentally, all her clothes were very nice.) The whole thing must have been a humiliating experience for them, and Peter and I thought, not without a certain satisfaction, there goes one American couple who will not go home and rhapsodize about the Soviet way of life.

It was 1:00 a.m. by the time we got home, and the flat was positively gleaming with cleanliness — good old Nina. We slept in late the following morning, but were able to attend a couple of cocktail parties in the evening, where it was very pleasant to be welcomed back enthusiastically by our diplomatic colleagues.

On Wednesday Vic and little John came to lunch, and on Thursday Vic went to Stockholm to fetch Kris and the new baby, and I became responsible for John until Vic's return. On Wednesday morning he was at school (he is six years old), but Thursday was already the Easter holidays, and I had him at home all day. He could not have been more pleasant, intelligent, and entertaining, but nevertheless I was so exhausted by evening that I had to go to bed at nine o'clock! The next day we were all going out to the airport to meet the returning ones at 3:00 p.m., but, alas, Vic phoned to say that they had not been able to get seats on the plane, and would not arrive until 11:20 p.m. This caused a mild crisis, but fortunately John recovered himself very quickly, and we were able to put in another day, which included a short rest for him and for me in the afternoon, which I think I needed far more than he did. At night he was much too excited to sleep, and not keen to be left alone, so the two of us lay in the dark of his bedroom and he talked and asked questions non-stop from 7:30 to 10:30. Then we were driven in the Embassy station wagon to the airport, and since the plane was a little delayed there was a long wait there, and poor tired John became more and more depressed and I think convinced himself that his mother was not going to come at all; in fact he said with a terrible adult bitterness: "*They* won't come." When finally they did arrive John was overjoyed, but no more so than Peter and I, who felt a huge load of responsibility slip from our shoulders. The baby was only ten days old, so naturally Kris was pretty exhausted, having been out of hospital only two days, but I saw her yesterday and she is now looking fine and the baby is said to be thriving.

On Saturday it was cold but sunny, and in the afternoon we drove out to the University with the Crowes and walked around it. By some extraordinary fluke we even managed to get inside without being stopped; the gremlin who was guarding the door was distracted just as we appeared and neglected her duty, for which I hope she doesn't get into trouble. We didn't prowl beyond the main halls, but we did see one detail of interest: there was a big illustrated placard about Hungary hanging in one place; part of it was devoted to photos of the destruction caused during what they called the *Contrarevolutcia*, only some daring person had scribbled over the "*Contra*."

That same evening we went with the Crowes to see a play, *Krilya*. The Crowes had read it and were able to help a lot (they understand Russian pretty well), so I got more out of it than I usually do. It had one quite entertaining scene where a stuffy professor is lecturing the members of a Tractor Station on the joys of total communism and they laugh at him and ask irreverent questions. Afterwards we tried to get into a restaurant, but all were full — in fact people were queuing for places *outside* the main door, in the cold street. There are no facilities for queuing inside. So we came home and ate caviar and drank vodka and tea.

On Sunday the Bishop celebrated communion (the Bishop of Fulham, that is, who was doing the rounds of his diocese of Northern Europe) and the Ambassador invited us to breakfast afterwards, which so confused his poor Sunday maid that she poured hot coffee into Peter's empty juice glass.

It was a cold, wet day, but we nevertheless followed our plan of doing a little trip. Carol, one of our nice stenos (they are all nice, actually), and Ann Knox, the Naval Attaché's wife, came to lunch and then we were driven to Archangelskoe, one of the splendid homes of the Usipov family. The thermometers in each of the rooms indicated a below-freezing temperature, so we didn't linger, but it was fun just to be there.

Monday was a holiday but Peter worked anyway. In the evening we went to a farewell cocktail party for the Bishop, who is young and extremely nice. And that brings you up to date.

Much love to you all,

Ever,

Nao.

⌁ ⌁

Moscow

15 April 1958

My dear Father,

We are delighted that you and Mother are thinking of paying us a visit here. I suggest that, if it is convenient for you, you arrange to come early in June, perhaps for about three weeks. We have a spare bedroom in our apartment and will of course expect you to occupy it while you're in Moscow.

If you plan to do any travelling outside Moscow during your stay, you will be able to make the arrangements through Intourist here. This applies also to any other facilities you may want to ask for, as a journalist or as a tourist.

We'll look forward to seeing you before long.

Affectionately,

Naomi.

⌁ ⌁

Moscow

20 April 1958

Dear Everybody,

Thank you for all your letters (from Ma Z., Liz, Pa Z., Mary, Pa R., dated in that order). All were interesting and much enjoyed.

This will be a quickie. I am doing a six-week stint in the kindergarten, and I find that my afternoons are not much good for literary composition after I have spent my mornings with twenty-six children in a much too small room surrounded by other rooms in which other teachers are trying to teach their classes long division.

So, the events since I last wrote, in brief:

On the 10th I made a little tour, with other Canadians and with my teacher, of the Novodevichy Monastery, which isn't as fine as Zagorsk as regards its buildings, but which has an even richer display of church possessions in its museum. The Church was undoubtedly too powerful and too wealthy for its own good before the Revolution. A priest's gown might be embroidered with a thousand real pearls and his crown encrusted with precious jewels of extravagant size, while his parishioners lived on potatoes. This seems like poor distribution.

On Friday (the Russian Good Friday) we saw *Giselle* at the Bolshoi, a memorable experience.

On Saturday Doris Crowe and I passed by a church where there was a line of Russians all carrying their little bundles consisting of an Easter loaf and a flower and eggs, all wrapped in a white cloth in a basket. We joined the line and were allowed to pass through the church and to have holy water splashed on us by the priest. All that day the streets were full of people carrying their loaves to church to be blessed; it seems to be a tradition even the most lukewarm are loath to ignore.

That night we went to a dinner party, and then the whole lot of us went on to join the midnight-to-4:00 a.m. celebrations at the Cathedral. The crowds trying to get into the church were thick, but the Diplomatic Corps very unfairly has a section reserved for it, from which it can gawp at the natives without being trodden underfoot by them. It is a moving service with haunting music, but it was rather spoiled by the slightly cocktail-party atmosphere in the Diplomats' enclosure.

On Tuesday we went to the opera *Eugene Onegin*, but I'm sorry to say that we were bored and left after the first act.

On Wednesday evening some staff showed in the Embassy the movie *The Desperate Hours*, borrowed from the British. We invited to join us the Russian young woman who works in the administrative office, and though she strongly disapproved of the non-educational, non-morally-uplifting theme, she finally acknowledged that the film had been absorbing and was well done. It wasn't a very good advertisement for the American way of life, but it was nevertheless the best movie we have been loaned during our seven months here.

On Thursday we went to a concert to hear the excellent Russian pianist Sviatoslav Richter play Schumann and Brahms. Peter says that the orchestra was well below the standard of the soloist, but it was still most enjoyable.

Yesterday (Saturday) we went for drinks to the Moores' in order to admire the new baby, and today our newly engaged Air Attaché's clerk and his fiancée are coming to supper, after which we will all go to the movie at America House (the easy way to entertain).

This brings you up to date, and I must go and prepare the supper. Apologies for the brevity.

Much love to you all, and I hope you are well.

Naomi.

Moscow
28 April 1958

Dear All,

Positively *no* letter today as it has been a very busy week, and anyway I am feeling glum, having started on my second cold since returning from London; had a blissful few weeks respite until now. Otherwise, all is going well.

We gave a very dreary small dinner party last Tuesday, and a successful cocktail party for sixty on Friday. For the latter Nina prepared delicious *zakouski*, the service was good, and the guests seemed quite to enjoy themselves. What a relief, after parties so dull as all our recent ones have been. We must give a big cocktail party for Ma and Pa when they come, as I hope they will.

There was a sequel to the saga concerning our (all right, my) carelessness in letting our sterling bank account run dry: the cheque that we sent off via the air hostess was unendorsed and had to be returned to us! In Canada one doesn't need to endorse a cheque to be paid into one's own account, and Peter forgot to do so. Meanwhile we had gaily written new cheques, drawing even further on our empty account. Is one of you standing bail for us?

Thanks for forwarding Peter's abominable snow boots, which safely arrived, but which, hooray, won't be needed again this year. We now have lots of rain but luckily no snow, and it is pleasantly warm.

I finally ran to earth a Moscow hairbrush for P. after a morning's search that caused quite a lot of interest, because I had not thought to look up the word, and had to act it out in each shop. The shopgirls and other customers entered into the spirit of the quest with great abandon.

We saw *Uncle Vanya* on Saturday and it was terrific. If you could read it first in English, I think you would enjoy the production when they bring it to London next month. Liz, next time you are near a Colletts bookstore would you pick up for me a catalogue of Russian plays in translation from which I could order some titles? I enjoy the plays so much more if I am not straining every nerve just to keep abreast of the plot. Usually it takes me the whole of the first act just to relate the different actors to their parts as described in the program.

Kindergarten is going pretty well, though tiring. Last week we made an Indian village, and on Friday I taught them to make paper mats by snipping at folded pieces of paper; great success.

Much love to you all,
Nao

—◦—◦—

Moscow
4 May 1958

Dear Family,

The Ambassador has just been entertaining thirty of Canada's million-aires, with our assistance. They include the presidents of Eaton's, Toronto-Dominion Bank, A.V. Roe, De Havilland, McLaughlin Construction Company, and so on ... They are on a tour, and even though they arrived only yesterday they are pretty dissatisfied with the way they are treated, and as one of them owns the *Toronto Globe and Mail* and another the *Toronto Telegram*, I imagine the Soviet Union will get a bad press.

Earlier in the week we entertained a young Canadian actor and his wife, who happens to be the daughter of the Speaker of the House of Commons; they had really been given the runaround by the Soviet authorities and were thoroughly cheesed off. They are a pleasant, intelligent, and well-mannered pair. However, when they were invited to lunch at the Ambassador's the young man wore a turtleneck sweater, for which the Ambassador is quite unable to forgive him, rather unfairly, I thought.

Nina has been away for nine days and I've been truly busy, especially as my mornings are occupied with kindergarten. Also, I am taking antihistamine and ephedrine to combat my persistent catarrh, and they make me feel low. The cocktails with the millionaires cheered me slightly, otherwise you would have had no letter today.

Poor Peter has been sent out to the airport to meet visiting Canadians for the second time this weekend. Being junior boy is a nuisance.

Much love,
N.

—◦—◦—

Moscow
9 May 1958

My dear Pa,

Thanks for your May Day letter. We look forward increasingly to your visit as the days go by, and think you will enjoy yourselves, even if you don't get much sensational news.

They are giving you a lot of hot air from this end. Thousands of ordinary tourists, not to mention journalists, come here every year without any invitation from anyone, and you can do the same. More important, we (as an Embassy and therefore as individuals) are not allowed to support the visa application of anyone except a Canadian official on business. This is why we did not put your invitations on official paper. Three days ago the Embassy refused to write to the Foreign Ministry on behalf of the daughter of the Speaker of the Canadian House of Commons, who was here and wanted to stay an extra few days. Sorry we can't do this for you, but to tell the truth I don't think it makes the least difference.

A long trip outside Moscow may well be impossible for you because of the expense, but I think we would be free to go to Leningrad with you, if you like, I for a weekend, Naomi for longer. I don't think it will be necessary to join a tour, but it may be convenient to hire an Intourist car and driver. I may write again in order to propose a possible trip to the Caucasus, because I am going there myself in about ten days time, intending to be away a week, and I shall soon have a good idea about costs, distances, and interest.

Your proposed date is good for us. I shall get back from my trip on May 25, and hope to leave on another trip on June 20; you will fit in between splendidly. The second trip is not yet confirmed, lacking as I do the Ambassador's permission, not to mention that of the Foreign Ministry.

Unfortunately the theatre and ballet season will have ended, probably, by the time you get here. If you arrive at the first of June, or just before, you might catch the last *Swan Lake* at the Bolshoi. Well worth catching too.

My life is all too full these days of very rich Canadian businessmen, thirty-two of them, about whom you must have read. We got them packed off to Leningrad today.

It is too late to go on chatting, especially as I shall see you in a few weeks.
Love to you all
Peter

Moscow
12 May 1958

My dear Parents,

I'm sorry the Soviet authorities have been leading you up the garden path. It would have been better, I think, simply to ask for a visa in the ordinary way, and wait until the application was refused (which was fairly unlikely to happen) before mentioning that you had relatives in the country. Now you are back at the beginning again, and I wonder if you can possibly have your arrangements made by June 1st.

If you expect to put the visit off a week or so, please do let me know, as I have been invited to participate in an "all-girls" trip, and I might be able to squeeze it in before your visit if you are delayed a few days.

You will want to know about clothes to bring. Pa should probably bring a DJ in case you are invited to a formal party, but Ma need not bring a long dress. The only criterion distinguishing a short evening dress from a short cocktail dress would seem to be a décolleté neckline. I think two silk dresses should see you through any parties to which you are invited — there may be none, other than those we give at home.

Would you please bring a present to keep Nina happy? A handbag might be an appropriate choice; anyway, something that *shows*, and can therefore be shown off. If you would bring some dress lengths of pretty material, I would gladly buy them from you, both for me and as presents for maids. That is something else that Nina would like, I think. Incidentally, she is size 40 and loves royal blue. Thank goodness she came back today after two weeks' sickness. Her absence has meant that I have been very busy.

No more now. Let us know your plans as soon as you can — by open mail, if you wish, so long as you are non-committal and don't tell them anything they don't already know.

Looking forward to seeing you both, and love to you and Liz,
N.

Moscow
18 May 1958

My dear Parents,

Poor you, what a bad time you are having as you try to obtain your visas. But perhaps by now all is well, for the Ambassador has agreed like a lamb to Peter's sending the sort of note that was needed, and it has been sent (last Friday). It says:

"The Canadian Embassy presents its compliments to the Ministry of Foreign Affairs of the USSR, and has the honour to inform the Ministry that the parents of Mrs P.M. Roberts, wife of the Second Secretary of the Embassy, propose to visit Moscow in June and to stay as the private guests of Mr and Mrs Roberts in their apartment in the Embassy. Mrs Roberts's parents are Mr and Mrs H.D. Ziman, of 10 Eton Road, London, England. They have already applied to the Soviet Embassy in London for visitors' visas. Mr and Mrs Roberts would be grateful if the Ministry would authorize the Soviet Embassy in London to issue the necessary visas as soon as possible."

Assuming that all goes well, we now expect you both from about June 7th to June 28th; is that right? Peter leaves for Murmansk on the 20th, but I shall stay behind and we can do lots of things together. I hope that we will be able to spend several days in Leningrad. There are also some one-day trips one can make from Moscow (though for no evident reason one or the other of these may suddenly be put out of bounds at the last minute).

Today I was driven with the girls of the Embassy office staff to Yasnaya Polyana, Tolstoy's home, about 190 km. away, and I found my spirits lifting with every kilometre we covered as we sped from Moscow. Suddenly summer has arrived, and the trees are at their most beautiful. But I must warn you (thinking of your travel wardrobes) that June last year was colder than May had been (so I am told). Yasnaya P. is very pleasant, and we must try to visit it while you are with us.

Peter left Moscow on Saturday, a day later than intended because there were no tickets available for the plane on Friday. He should be back on Monday May 26, and his itinerary is: Stalingrad — Makhachkala — Baku — Tbilisi — Mineralni Vodi — Moscow. Lucky man.

An hour ago Betsy Barnes rang up to confirm her invitation to me to join her and another American wife on a four-day trip by personal car to Rostov and Yaroslavl. Betsy is the wife of Harry Barnes, a U.S. diplomat (both extremely likeable and well informed), and her companion is Tobi Frankel, wife of Max Frankel, the no. 2 man of the *New York Times* in Moscow. If I can find a substitute-substitute teacher for the kindergarten I will accept like a shot. It is high time that I began to travel a little, and these two would be delightful companions, curious and enterprising, and fairly fluent in Russian. I feel honoured to be invited, given how many American wives there are whom they might have chosen to join them.

Much love,

N.

⌒ ⌒

Moscow
29 May 1958

My dear Ma, Pa and Liz,

Sorry, no letter this week; the bag is leaving on *Friday* and I am leaving today for a four-day trip (Yaroslavl and Rostov, north of Moscow). I heard from P. in Baku last night that all is well. He should be in Tbilisi by now.

I do hope that your visas have come through and that you have not given up the idea of visiting us in Moscow.

Goodbye for now,

Love,

Nao.

⌒ ⌒

Moscow
24 June 1958

My dear Liz,

The parents find Moscow gloomy and oppressive. They also feel some-what at a loss by virtue of not knowing the language and not having a city map (wouldn't we all like one of those?). You know how well they nor-mally navigate cities new to them? This time, no. However, they have bravely gone out on their own several times, and kind strangers have come to their rescue when they seemed in need.

At social events (given by us or others) we have introduced them to a few select members of the diplomatic corps and of the foreign press corps from among our acquaintances. Most of these contacts have provided Pa with useful background information.

At the Queen's Birthday cocktail party at the British Embassy Sir Patrick Reilly kindly made sure that Pa was introduced to some of the Big Boys. Pa was able to have a superficial conversation with Mikoyan and a longer talk with Khrushchev (through an interpreter, of course). Pa says it was not front-page stuff but will work well in a feature article.

Many colleagues have offered hospitality and assistance to our guests, among them David Mark, who invited Pa and Ma to join a group on a visit to the State Rooms of the Kremlin, an event that the Americans had been trying for a year to set up.

In our company the parents have seen *Swan Lake* at the Stanislavsky Theatre, and on their own they went to see a visiting French ballet troupe perform at the Bolshoi. They toured the Pushkin Museum (a nice art gallery) and we all made an excursion to see the Monastery of Zagorsk, where religious practice is permitted and the buildings were packed with worshippers. Pa also visited the Lenin State Library and was taken on a tour of a factory and another tour of a collective farm. I expect he will be writing about all these experiences.

Now we have just returned from Leningrad, a city that Pa and Ma great-ly preferred to Moscow. For me too it was refreshing to get out of Moscow and to be in such a handsome city. We must try to arrange for you to see it when you come. Peter could stay only for the weekend, and anyway was suffering from Leningrad tummy, so I am afraid he did not profit much from the trip, but he hopes to pay another visit some day.

We stayed in an Intourist hotel and had the same experiences that tourists so often complain about: slow service (e.g., a one hour's wait for breakfast after we had placed our order), reluctant and/or officious staff, absence of bath and handbasin stoppers, etc. On the other hand, the bedrooms are palatial and the public rooms are on the grand scale. Privileged Russians travelling abroad must find the hotel accommodation of Western Europe strangely meagre.

The weather was decidedly cool for mid-June. Poor Ma felt chilled all day while we toured Peterhof, in spite of the fact that she was wearing a blouse, cardigan, jacket, and raincoat! Peterhof is in the throes of restoration, having been much destroyed by the Germans; consequently we were not able to see inside the Palace, but we were able to admire the building from the outside. We strolled in the Versailles-style grounds among fountains and gilded statues. (Ma thought that Midas had run riot there.) I want to follow up on our visit by finding out more about Peter the Great and his age.

On another day we visited the Hermitage. Even Pa recognized that he could not see in the course of one day every room and every item on display. In fact we spent only three hours there, but were able to take away a strong impression of the stunning rooms and the amazing collections. The parquet floors alone were a sight to behold.

Somehow or other we were granted permission to be shown some of the degenerate art of the twentieth century (Picasso et al.), which is concealed from the eyes of vulnerable Soviet citizens in a locked area. I suppose the premise is that foreigners are already corrupt so cannot be harmed by exposure to these paintings. An elderly woman curator took great pleasure in showing us painting after painting, all of which she clearly admired and appreciated. The canvases are well preserved and are easily accessible, stored vertically like kitchen trays. One can only assume that the museum experts are aware of the value of modern abstract art and are waiting patiently until regime attitudes change. Good for them.

Perhaps this letter will reach you only after the parents' return. You will in any case hear from them a much fuller account of our activities than I have given you. I hope they feel it was a successful visit. I know they were often tired and discouraged.

Your turn next!

Much love,

Naomi.

Moscow
29 June 1958

My dear Parents,

I hope you are safely home; I imagine that we would have been told if anything had gone amiss.

We were fairly tired at the end of your three-week visit, but I should think nothing like as exhausted as you must have felt. Too bad that all the opportunities for interviews, etc., turned up toward the end of your stay, so that you were kept running from appointment to appointment, with scarcely time for you to give us your report on each one. But all in all, I was pleased with the way the visit went, and felt that you were both profiting from the scraps of information that were thrown your way, and the glimpses of Soviet life that were revealed. I hope you feel this way too. We are all agog to see the articles. I certainly don't envy you the writing of them.

By the way, did you experience that feeling of elation that we have told you about once you were out of range of any possible listening devices? The need to monitor one's every utterance probably sounds to most people like a minor inconvenience, but as you may have discovered even after a mere three weeks, this self-censorship weighs heavily and increasingly as time goes by. One really only becomes fully aware of the pressure once one is relieved of it.

Greetings from the Moores and from the Crowes, who were all sorry not to say goodbye to you in person.

As usual, no comment from the maids or from Maya as to whether they liked their presents. I will try to provoke a response when the opportunity arises.

Peter played volleyball all yesterday afternoon in a Canada versus America match and is almost too stiff to move today. But apart from this, we are fully rested and recovered from all the excitements of the last month. I feel sorry for Ma having to return to housework after her un-holiday.

Love to Liz and to you both, and I hope you don't have any evil after-effects resulting from your Russian visit. (This sounds sinister, but I was not referring to political after-effects.)

Ever,

Nao.

Moscow
11 July 1958

My dear Parents,

Thank you for your two letters in the last bag and for the cutting from the *Sunday Express*, which we found quite amusing. We intend to go looking for the American bar in the Peking one day.

Our National Day party was quite pleasant, largely because most of the invited Russian bigwigs cut it (though we did get Mikoyan), and there was consequently lots of room for the guests to move around. Doris and I did the flowers, not very well, I thought, and we all acted the gracious host or hostess. Peter stood most of the time under a great bouquet held together (I hope invisibly) by string and scotch tape, and directed the guests upstairs. People told me that the bouquet was very becoming to him. Among the guests was Malcolm Muggeridge, who kissed me fondly and said kind things.

Kris was not present at the party, and we learned subsequently that she was horribly ill, in fact for several days she was in a critical state. She had developed food-poisoning after eating in a restaurant and as a result of this her stomach ulcer perforated. I spent a lot of time last week running errands or just standing by in order to relieve Vic, who did all the nursing himself, including feeding her intravenously and operating a draining machine whose name I don't remember. Thank goodness, she has turned the corner now and is recovering daily, though she is still very weak, of course.

We haven't had our Hungarian and Austrian bookings confirmed yet, but if all goes well we expect to spend the nights of the 25th and 26th July in Budapest and the 27th July to the 7th August (or possibly longer) in Vienna or elsewhere in Austria. Yes, please, we would indeed like to borrow your Baedeker on Austria.

The only parties we have been to since you left were the American National Day reception and a dinner plus movie at the home of the American Assistant Air Attaché. Oh, yes, and there was a small cocktail party given by Sir Patrick and Lady Reilly for the ten Moscow teachers and students who are going to Oxford for a summer course. We gave your name and address to a delightful teacher called Mrs Nathan, who might just possibly call you, though I doubt it rather. We must try not to let slip this tenuous connection, but invite her here when the group returns.

All I could find to give Peter for his birthday was a balalaika, which is more decorative than musical, but I expect we will be doing lots of shopping in Vienna.

Please thank Liz for her letter. Love to her and to you,

Naomi.

P.S. Lots of people enquire after you.

The Canadian Embassy in Moscow, 23 Starokonyushenny Pereulok.

The "Domik" in the Embassy compound, home to the Counsellor and his family.

The Ziman parents
(a few years later)
ready to welcome
visitors to 10 Eton
Road.

Elizabeth Ziman
with her sister
Naomi.

Frank and Muriel
Roberts at home.
Mary Roberts
accompanies her
mother as she
boards a TCA flight
to join Peter and
Naomi on holiday.

A 1958 delegation of Canadian business leaders is greeted at Moscow airport. Peter Roberts is keeping an eye on proceedings. (Courtesy of *Maclean's.*)

The Chargé d'Affaires and Mrs. Roberts are invited to a reception offered by the Emperor of Ethiopia …

BY COMMAND OF

HIS IMPERIAL MAJESTY
HAILE SELASSIE 1ST EMPEROR OF ETHIOPIA

THE AMBASSADOR OF ETHIOPIA
HAS THE HONOUR TO REQUEST THE ATTENDANCE OF

The Chargé d'Affaires of Canada and Mrs. P.M. Roberts

AT A RECEPTION TO BE GIVEN BY HIS IMPERIAL MAJESTY
AT THE KREMLIN PALACE

ON *Friday* THE *10th* OF *July* 1959, AT *18 hours*

IN HONOUR OF

HIS EXCELLENCY K. E. VOROSHILOV
PRESIDENT OF THE PRESIDIUM OF THE SUPREME SOVIET OF THE U.S.S.R.

В честь Его Величества Хайле Селассие I, Императора Эфиопии

Президиум Верховного Совета СССР
Правительство
Союза Советских Социалистических Республик

просят г. П.М. Робертса, Временного Поверенного
в Делах Канады, с супругой

пожаловать на приём

11 июля 1959 г. в 16 час. 00 мин.

Большой Кремлёвский Дворец.

… and to a reception in honour of His Majesty in July 1959.

Peter and Naomi stand in front of their apartment windows, ready to greet guests in the Embassy garden on Canada Day 1959.

Victor Moore and his family after their return to Ottawa in 1958.

Max and Janice Yalden attend a skating party at the British Embassy.

Carol and Blair Seaborn with Virginia and Geoffrey at the Costakis dacha, with their hosts George and Zina Costakis and two of their children.

Doris Crowe with Naomi and her mother at Zagorsk in June 1958.

Marshall Crowe

Nina, cook-maid for the
Roberts's, poses for them in
the Embassy garden.

Nikolai, senior driver for the
Embassy staff. (The other
drivers are Dima II and Ilya;
the Ambassador has his own
driver, Dima I.)

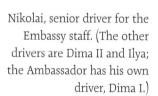

George Costakis, local administrator and art collector, in his office (after work hours).

The Ambassador's table is laid and the domestic staff is ready to serve his guests on Christmas Day, 1957.

A gift shop on
the Boulevards.

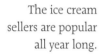

The ice cream
sellers are popular
all year long.

Pedestrians are
many, cars are
few in Moscow
streets.

It must be springtime; we have put aside our winter headgear.

Arbat Square, Naomi's shopping district.

Outside the Old Believers' Church.

Country children permit
the foreign visitors to
take pictures of them.

Young Pioneers in Kiev.

In the Ukraine, January 1959. Max Yalden has come to identify some army pensioners who served Canada during the First World War.

Gypsies in Makhachkala (Dagestan), viewed from Peter's hotel window in May 1958.

Yaroslavl

Some young people in Rostov
examine the foreign car
which has brought three
strangers to their city in
July 1958.

Rostov

Moscow
20 July 1958

My dear Parents,

Yes, okay, okay, I will have an X-ray, though I assure you I do not have TB. I now have a letter addressed to the Polyclinic and I will go along there, perhaps tomorrow. Thank you for your concern anyway, though I feel sure it is unnecessary. As expected, Peter did not go to see the doc about the troubles he had experienced in Leningrad, but I described to him (the doc) all the symptoms, and he thought it sounded like nervous cramps rather than anything intestinal, which had been my diagnosis too. A holiday should help.

Well now, thank you for the lovely bundle of birthday surprises in celebration of my 29th birthday and of Peter's 31st. The magazines have all been gloated over, we both use P.'s hairbrush because it is so super, and the blouse is very handsome. I cleverly contrived to unwrap the white handbag in front of Nina and said, "Oh, my mother knew I admired the one she gave you, and so she has sent me one as a birthday present." Nina rose to the bait and said yes, it was very nice and to thank my mother from her. Oh, the lengths we will go to in order to get a response.... It was an exciting parcel, and thank you for everything.

Sorry that Pa is having difficulty with his articles, but I am not a bit surprised. I think Ma's idea about offering a talk on *Woman's Hour* is a good one, and I make her a present of any story I have ever told in a letter (except where it concerns our Embassy or any other one), though it might be best to check with me first in case I have exaggerated.

Here is another story for you. In the market on Saturday the international tension was relieved slightly when a kolkhozian woman from whom I had bought carrots conferred with her pal and then called me back to say *"Vwee nam nravitze"* — i.e., "We like you," or, more accurately, "You delight us."

Usually they make their personal remarks in front of you but not *to* you, like the old biddy who stuck her head through the open window of Betsy Barnes's car when Betsy and Tobi and I were sitting there and said, "Look at the three pretty girls." When I obediently looked at her three elderly companions I was rather surprised at her description of them, then realized that it was they who were supposed to be admiring us.

During that trip we had an agreeable encounter with a merry group of young peasant women who returned from work in a farm truck just as we paused in their village.

"How do you like our village?" they asked us.

"Very much," of course we replied.

I was afraid that they would follow up by asking us what in particular we liked. As we could identify only a muddy, unpaved road with a yellow mongrel dog lying in it, we would have found it hard to respond in a positive way. I suppose we would have chimed: "Lyudi!" (the people), but luckily the women appeared satisfied with our only comment on their home and then questioned us about ourselves. What cheery, uncomplaining people they are.

The other day a crowd in the market was silently studying Doris and me and the Embassy car when Doris addressed one of them with a question. They could not have looked more astonished. "Look, it can speak too."

Much love,
Naomi.

———— ∙~∙ ————

Moscow
22 July 1958

My dear Lethbridge and London families,

Apart from the vicarious excitement of demonstrations held in front of other embassies we have had a quiet week. A boat-ride party to which we were going last night, a big affair, was cancelled at the last minute when the Russians withdrew their permission for the hire of the boat — just to annoy, I suppose. The poor young host, the son of one of the British diplomats, sounded almost tearful with disappointment.

On Sunday we took a little walk in Gorki Park and watched the populace enjoying its holiday peacefully. "Spontaneous" demonstrations take place only during working hours, when the indignant crowd is duly paid for being indignant. Nina summed it up nicely when Peter asked her jokingly on Friday why she wasn't at the demonstration, and she replied tartly that she hadn't been invited.

Kris made a remarkable recovery and is in circulation again, in fact we are giving a big farewell cocktail party for her and Vic on Wednesday. We are still undecided as to whether to move out to their apartment, but I think we will probably stay where we are, as being less trouble than moving and adjusting to a new life. Personally I enjoy being able to do most of my outdoor tasks on foot and not requiring the use of an Embassy car and driver.

Nina has been very sweet-tempered and willing lately, and works like a horse. So I made her a speech, telling her that she had worked for me for nearly a year and I was pleased with her work; I therefore wanted her to choose for herself, as a present, a dress from the latest Eaton's catalogue. "So how much money do I have to give you?" asks Nina suspiciously. After having been twice assured that the dress will be a present "without payment," she comments, "You are three times crazy." However, she marched off with the catalogue, very pleased, and let me measure her next day. But at the last minute she blushed and asked, pointing to her bust, "Are you going to measure me here? Just a minute, then." She darted off downstairs, and came back looking a different woman, obviously having put on her bra, which she takes off when she starts work. (I think all the maids do this; bras have no elastic and are not comfortable for all-day wear.)

Another domestic detail that I have noticed recently is that, presumably as a result of the universal use of the abacus, the market men and women are just hopeless at mental arithmetic. The decimal system should not cause many problems, but if one buys 600 grams of something at 8 roubles a kilo, every neighbouring kolkhozian, plus a crowd of idle customers, is called upon to help work out the sum. We Canadians create a problem by bringing little plastic pots to be filled (no one has any wrapping material to give away). The sellers weigh the pot first and leave the corresponding weights on the balance side of the scales, so that they will not have to deduct the amount from the total purchase. The snag is that the plastic is so light that it is hard to find a true counterbalance among the conventional weights. The market people are scrupulously accurate, and so it may happen that I end up with a rag and three strawberries as the counterbalance to my plastic pot.

Another sight that amuses me is an old kolkhoz woman who has to find change for 100 roubles; invariably, up go her skirts and out of her voluminous bloomers comes a little bundle of grey and greasy banknotes adding up to one hundred! (Sorry if this puts you off your food. It doesn't bother me, for it is such a treat to be able to buy fresh fruit that I would endure much worse in order to make the purchase.)

We are off on our holiday early on Friday morning and will be gone about two weeks. The Embassy in Vienna would be a good place to get in touch with us if you need to do so. We will write to you from Austria.

Much love to you all,

Naomi.

Altmunster-am-Traumsee
Salzkammergut Austria
9 August 1958

My dear Family,

We thought when we got here last Friday that, lovely as the place was, our joy was at an end. Everything had been so splendid up to then, Budapest and Vienna, and here we found ourselves in a very poor (albeit very cheap) hotel on a noisy main highway, with the worst weather of the summer just beginning. But the quality of the hotel as it turned out was not important, since we were scarcely ever in it, and the weather, after a day or two of catastrophic storms throughout the Salzkammergut, turned into the best possible for a holiday, and with two days more to go in these parts we are having a very good time indeed. We return to Vienna on Thursday, and after a final fling there head for Moscow on Saturday.

People who inflict on other people detailed accounts of their holidays are not to be tolerated, generally speaking. But I want to write down before I forget it all that we have seen and heard and done on this holiday, especially the Budapest part, and I know you won't mind being the audience. Not that anything very astonishing happened, but it's a pity to go to an interesting and relatively unvisited country like Hungary without adding one's impression to the general store of knowledge. Needless to say, our two and a half days in Budapest were by far the most interesting of the days we have been away from Moscow, and in many ways they were the best holiday too. Hungary hasn't been "building socialism" for long, which means there are still many of what the Russians call "hangovers of capitalism," and therefore, for the Western visitor, the means of leading quite a pleasant life. This does not, alas, hold true for the miserable inhabitants.

I have a hunch that our impressions of Hungary are different from and in a way more valuable than those of ordinary Western visitors, because we came there direct from a year of living in a country where socialism has been completely built, and where the inhabitants, except the old, remember only the present universal dreariness. Hungary is deceptive and frustrating, because the Soviet way has not yet informed the life that one sees in the streets and shops and restaurants, and one forgets that the method of government is the same as that in the Soviet Union, but even more repulsive. People are poor and they live crowded like fleas on a dog, but they maintain an extraordinary dignity, beautiful manners, and (despite impossible shortages) an astounding sense of style in their dress. Just as they come they are probably the most handsome race in Europe, their colouring ranging between extremes of blond and quite dark, displaying lithe muscular bodies of which they are extremely proud. Their simple and stylish clothing makes them even more attractive.

Budapest is a fine city, but not interesting as regards picture galleries, museums, or antiquities (except a few Roman ones, which the Hungarians have ruined by trying to reconstruct). This is a great relief, for without feeling obliged to do any sightseeing, one can quietly enjoy the streets and buildings, still elegant in spite of a lot of war and revolution damage. The Parliament Buildings (as they facetiously call them) are grotesque — a copy of Westminster, I think — but not in a really disagreeable way. The Danube runs through the middle of the city, making some graceful curves; on the left bank is Buda, mainly residential and built on a series of low hills, and on the right is Pesht (correct pronunciation), which is flat and contains the main buildings of the city. Buda and Pesht were separate towns up to about 1850, I think.

The most attractive part of the town is a large island in the Danube called Margaret Island, devoted entirely to park. The few buildings on it, with one notable exception, were put there to help the people disport themselves on a Sunday afternoon: swimming pools filled with naturally warm mineral water, cafés, a small stadium (where the world wrestling championships were taking place while we were visiting the city), and the like. The notable exception was the hotel where we stayed, a beautiful place, if decaying somewhat, surrounded by gardens and woods and river, still well run, with a good restaurant and bar where you can buy Seagrams V.O. as well as vodka. Our room, like many others, had a large balcony overlooking the garden, closed above and on the windward side, so you could sit there pleasantly even if it rained (which it didn't during our stay). We had our breakfast there every morning in the sunshine, and marvelled that life could be so pleasant in a Communist country. Alas, it is all capitalistic hangovers, and if the regime ever succeeds in rooting these out, Hungary will be as sad a place as the Soviet Union. But there is a lot of rooting out to be done before that stage is reached.

It seems to be harder for Westerners to make contact with Hungarians in Budapest than with Russians in Moscow. Many Russians, especially those outside Moscow, don't realize the dangers of contact with foreigners, and they are in any case immensely curious about "abroad," and starved for information, so they are willing to take a chance. The regime in the Soviet Union feels pretty secure these days, and I imagine the consequences of a casual conversation with a travelling Western diplomat or tourist aren't very drastic. But in Hungary the regime feels anything but secure, it knows that it is detested by ninety percent of the people it rules, and it fears, probably with reason, that it is actively plotted against. So it goes hard with a Hungarian who has contact with Westerners, and this is getting worse rather than better. According to our Western diplomatic acquaintances, the relaxation that followed the Revolution in 1956 is all but over. The secret police has been overhauled and is beginning to crack down. The result, of course, is that no Hungarian in his right mind would risk a serious contact with a foreigner. The hard thing about this for the newcomer to Budapest is that Hungarians look like people whom normally one would get to know. They look like Frenchmen or Englishmen or Swedes, and dress like them, except rather more stylishly. So it's very odd to realize that not only friendship but also even passing acquaintance is impossible. Russians don't look or act like anyone else — they can be wonderful people but always very different — and one therefore does not expect to chum up with them. In fact, a casual conversation is probably easier in Moscow than in Budapest.

In spite of all this, we got a small idea of what's going on in people's heads. True, most of our information came from a highly suspect source, an Ibusz guide. Ibusz is the Hungarian equivalent of the Soviet Intourist, an organization that, in Russia, controls from minute to minute the life of every foreign visitor to the country. In Hungary things are mercifully less well arranged. One arrives and goes to a hotel as in any country; Ibusz only lurks in the background and performs if called upon. The Ibusz and Intourist men are in contact with the secret police, who are informed of one's movements, but in the Soviet Union they have nevertheless often been known to speak about the regime with extraordinary frankness, and this proved to be so in Budapest too.

Our Ibusz man, who was spidery and apologetic, but pleasant, offered first to take us on a tour of the city by taxi. When we objected to the price, he at once suggested that we wait half an hour until he would come off duty, and then let him take us on a private enterprise tour by bus and streetcar. We would pay what we thought it was worth. Of course we accepted his proposal. The tour was interesting if exhausting, but of more interest were the guide's opinions about the state of things in Hungary. The 1956 "mess," as he called it, had certainly been a spontaneous and general uprising throughout the whole country, inspired by grave dissatisfaction with the regime, great hardship, and strong anti-Russian feeling. But when "Fascist elements" came in, the revolutionaries committed excesses, and if they had been allowed to continue thousands of innocent people would have suffered. It was not only the AVF who were hanged, he said, as he pointed to the famous tree on which victims were hanged, but also many who were guilty of nothing. So the Russian intervention, bad as it seemed at the time, was after all a good thing. At the beginning, the Revolution was a time of great hope for everyone, he said. People thought that, without losing any of the benefits of socialism, they were about to rid themselves of a vicious government and a Russian occupation. The latter was an insane hope. Part of the fault certainly lay with the Americans, who led the Hungarians to think that Western help would be forthcoming if an uprising began. Even so, some good might have been done even without American help, had the "Fascist elements" not come in. Who were these Fascist elements? we asked. Were they American agents, or expatriate Horthyites slipped over the border, or were they people living in Hungary and waiting their chance? He didn't know who they were, of course.

The execution of Nagy and Maleter had shocked all Hungarians, our guide said. He himself, who had served under Maleter in the army, thought it a mistake. Of course they were both guilty; one mustn't be blinded to Maleter's faults on account of his excellence as a soldier. Nevertheless, they should not have been executed. The guide refused to comment on the possibility that the executions had been ordered not in Budapest but in Moscow.

About the Russians he spoke his mind eloquently. Every week, he said, we bid another solemn farewell to Russian soldiers going home, but the number of them never seems any smaller. In fact Naomi and I saw very few Soviet troops in Budapest, perhaps not more than a dozen, all obviously on leave and looking very isolated. Only two had managed to find girlfriends, and these looked so much like Russian women and so little like Hungarians that we speculated whether the Russian army, like the French, brings its own women when it goes to occupy a country. I don't know how many Hungarians speak Russian, but we found only one who admitted to it, and she was a little suspect, as I will tell you later. The Russian position in Hungary was symbolized for us by these hot, sweating Soviet soldiers in their wool uniforms and great thick boots, tramping the Budapest streets while the Hungarians, clean, cool, and fastidious, ignored them quite.

We saw the Russians in one other role while we were there. As I said, the world wrestling championships (or perhaps the European championships) were taking place in the small stadium not far from our hotel.

One night rather late as we were returning to the hotel, two Soviet wrestlers got on our bus when it stopped near the stadium. They were carrying a large bronze sculpture of two men wrestling, so heavy that they could just manage it between them. They glared sullenly at everyone during the bus journey, then staggered with the sculpture into the hotel, where they were also presumably staying. At the door I asked them if they were the champions. They said they were and I congratulated them, and would have gone on with the conversation had they been willing. They weren't, and went heaving up the stairs with their trophy. It seemed odd that the champs should have to take their trophy home on a bus, but on thinking it over I decided that the Hungarians would take some pleasure in handing two hundred pounds of bronze to the Soviet victors and leaving them to deal with it however they could.

To return to the Ibusz guide, he of course took the official line most of the time. Things are better now, he said, and the excesses of Stalinist days are over. (This is the reverse of what we were told by Westerners, who said that things are getting worse and life more difficult for the Hungarians, who will soon be living under something approaching another Stalinist terror.) What the guide said, and that doubtless was true, was that he was a quiet man, who believed in anything for a quiet life. Hanging and shooting were not his cup of tea. During the revolution he spent eight days in his cellar while the battle raged outside, and he never wants another time like that. Most Hungarians, he maintained, are of the same opinion. I think he is probably right, as long as the Russians are there. This generation of Hungarians has learned its lesson the hard way.

One of the nice things about Budapest is that (rare among Communist capitals) there are still a few good restaurants, many pleasant little bars where you can hear good music, and even a nightclub. We didn't try the nightclub, which is meant only for foreign tourists, we were told, but we did find the best-known restaurant, Gundel's, excellent, with wonderful service in the old manner, good Hungarian food and wines. We dined there twice, in the open air, with an orchestra playing discreet gypsy music. Twice we ventured into the little bars, and each time had a mildly interesting encounter. In the first bar, a respectable one, a man who seemed to be the manager (bars, like most things, are owned by the state) asked us if we knew Bill Johnson in the American Legation in Budapest. He has been my comrade for ten years, said the man. This seemed odd, because no American diplomat would have remained ten years in Budapest, but we asked an American friend next day if there were such a person. No, and never had been, to his knowledge. A minor mystery. The second bar was less respectable. It was full of smoke and fumes and American jazz and young Hungarian Teddy-boys and their girls jiving and drinking. It was about 1:00 a.m. when we went there, and we danced a bit and then sat up at the bar. The girl behind the bar, after some preliminaries, said she had a "very big question" to ask us, but we must wait until the boss's wife had left. So we waited, and presently the boss's wife did leave. The girl asked us if we could take a letter to her friend and mail it outside Hungary. We didn't say we either would or would not, but said we would be back the next day. The conversation then went on to other things, but haltingly, because we were speaking German and the girl was not fluent. Presently I tried her in Russian, and unlike all the other Hungarians with whom I had tried to converse in Russian, she responded at once and spoke very well. We thought over her request after we had left the bar, and decided that although it wasn't very likely to be a trap, it might be, and we had better leave it alone. So, somewhat regretfully, we didn't go back next day. The girl could not have been planted there especially for us, because no one knew that we were going into that bar until we came to the door. Besides, we were sure that we were not followed at all during our stay. However, it might be that she had orders to try this stunt on all foreigners, who, if they agreed to carry the letter, would perhaps find themselves carrying "state secrets" and liable to arrest and embarrassment.

A final, more rewarding, encounter was with the night clerk of our hotel, a well-educated man of about fifty-five, obviously a dispossessed bourgeois who had been lucky enough to be given a job as a clerk instead of being sent to prison. When he saw from our passports that we were Canadians, he said that he had a daughter and son-in-law in Winnipeg. They left in 1956, during the Revolution. I asked if there were any message he would like to send them, should I have a chance, and he said he would be glad if I could tell them that the family was getting on all right and they were not in trouble. He often wrote this to them, but felt that they thought he was afraid to write anything else. So he wrote down their name and former address in Winnipeg (they had recently moved and he didn't know the new address), and as soon as we got to Vienna I sent off these details to an old friend Alf Hosking, asking him to find the people and deliver the message.

During our time in Budapest the British Chargé d'Affaires, John Street, was extremely kind to us. I rang him up first thing and he at once offered to take us out with him and his wife and small daughter for a picnic lunch at the American club. We had a very happy afternoon with them there, and liked all three greatly. Naomi and Mrs Street found they had been at the same Oxford college, and we were generally much in harmony with them. The American club is a thing which the Americans in their enterprising way built for themselves and select fellow-foreigners when life for diplomats in Budapest became too confined. They bought or leased a war-ruined house and several acres of ground high up in the Buda hills, with a magnificent view of the Danube and over most of the city. They converted the ruin to a tiny but most attractive clubhouse with changing rooms and a bar and a card room, made the grounds into a minute golf course of only four holes (but quite difficult, they told us), and built for the children and non-golfers a pretty garden where one can sit to drink or eat, and a small but adequate swimming pool. They also managed to squeeze in a tennis court. All this, I believe, was done with private funds; the State Department had no hand in it.

The Streets and some of the other diplomats we met at this club told us something about their life in Budapest and about conditions generally. They are prevented from having contact with Hungarians in much the same way as we are with Russians, possibly more so. However, they are seldom followed by the secret police, although they drive their own cars, and they are not restricted at all in their movements around the country. I think you know that we are not allowed to go more than 40 kilometres outside Moscow without giving forty-eight hours notice to the Foreign Ministry, and there are huge areas in the Soviet Union where we are not allowed to go at all; also we are not allowed to leave Moscow by car on any but the two or three approved roads. In Budapest they have none of this, and it is quite possible for them to have a fairly pleasant holiday inside the country, although that is not usually necessary, as they are only four hours drive from Vienna, or fifty minutes by plane. But things are stiffening up, they told us. The secret police, which had to be completely rebuilt after the Revolution, is now finding its feet, and there are enough people to spare to watch the diplomats. So according to the Streets and their colleagues, life is getting tougher for the Western colony as well as for the wretched Hungarians.

Leaving Budapest when the time came was a bit of a problem, for there was no plane to Vienna that day, no sleepers on the night train, and no bus at all. However, John Street cleverly fixed this by getting us a ride with the wife of the American first secretary, who was going to Vienna on her six-weekly shopping spree (for food, mostly). It was an interesting ride, because we followed exactly the same route that thousands of refugees had followed during the Revolution, and we crossed the frontier at the same place, into the little Austrian village of Nikelsdorf, which, with a normal population of a few hundred, suddenly found itself host to many thousands of refugees who had just walked 150 miles carrying their children. The Austrians rose very well to the occasion. When we expressed surprise that so many people could have walked so far, Mrs Squire said dryly that "their adrenaline was flowing," which was about it. Our last sight of Hungary was the frontier: electrified barbed wire, plowed strip, guards with machine guns, and all the rest. A rabbit couldn't cross it now, although I'm told that a very occasional Hungarian does still make it across. At the time of the Revolution, the border guards simply waved the people through.

There is not much to tell about the Austrian part of our holiday, which was quiet and pleasant, and expensive — at least in Vienna. We stayed there for the first few days, shopping and sightseeing, visiting the wonderful wine cellars in Grinzing, where you sit in the garden sipping the local wine (very heady) and listening to a zither or accordion, while around you people sing sentimental Viennese songs. It's all very gentle and romantic. We looked for and found the place where the zither-player performs who won fame for his haunting rendition of the theme music of *The Third Man* movie. But it was "closed on account of holidays," which Naomi says is typically Austrian — tourist attractions are closed just as the tourists arrive, for Austrians like to enjoy their summer holidays too. As a matter of fact, the city seemed to be surprisingly free of tourists; perhaps they were all at lakeside resorts.

After a few days we went to the place where I started writing this letter (I am back in Moscow now, of course), and in spite of a poor hotel we had a very good time, walking in wonderful scenery and enjoying the local wine cellars in the evening. No American or British tourists to be seen, but quite a few French and German and Swiss. One day during this part of the holiday we made a day trip to Salzburg and there paid our respects to Mozart's birthplace, a rather fine house in the middle of the old part of the city. The Mozarts lived only on the top floor, I think, but it was as big as a modern luxury apartment. We had already visited the house where Beethoven lived, in Heiligestadt near Vienna, and therefore felt virtuous about our association with the great composers. We left Altmuenster just as the weather went sour last Thursday and returned to Vienna by train for another day and two nights of civilization before returning to Moscow on August 9th. Altogether it was a very satisfactory holiday.

We came back to a rather changed Embassy. Moores have gone for good, and Yaldens won't arrive till September 4th. The Ambassador, whose term has been extended by one or two years (we are glad), is going to Canada on home leave at the end of the month and won't be back until November. Meanwhile Marshall Crowe will be Chargé d'Affaires. We are beginning to think of the Moscow winter already and are determined to compensate as much as we can for its bleakness. In six weeks from now we shall have been here a full year, that is, half of our posting.

Love to you all,

Peter.

Addendum from Naomi: For the last few pages (you can easily detect the starting-point) I, Naomi, have been typing this from Peter's rough draft. It is now Monday and he is at work but wanted this to come to you in today's bag. The only snag is that this has left me no time to write my own letter to you, but I will get started on one tomorrow. Meanwhile, thank you for a pile of letters waiting for us in Moscow, and one from Father R. that *did* catch us in Vienna, so I hope he had put a big sum of money on his bet. I sent you postcards, not by airmail, from the airport in Budapest; let me know if they ever arrive.

(To the Ziman family: this is a copy of Peter's letter to the Robertses; not for public consumption, of course.)

— ~ —

Moscow

13 August 1958

My dear Pa,

What a pity one has to come back from Austria and start attending these infernal cocktail parties again. God, how I hate them. Tonight the party is chez our own Posol, in honour of some Canadian astronomers.

I am writing to thank you for your prompt and useful action in response to my request for information on different makes of car and their respective prices. We are studying the literature.

Your articles have just reached us but I haven't had time for a good look at them yet. I think from a quick glance that I shall like numbers 1 and 3 but not number 2. However, it is too early to give you a considered opinion.

I doubt that the Crowes have any immediate plans for coming to London since the fares were raised. Cost of taking the Crowe family to London and back is now about eight hundred and fifty pounds, which not even Canadian diplomats can afford.

Again, many thanks and love to you all. Please tell Liz that the note about her forthcoming visit has gone to the Ministry.

Peter.

———

Moscow
16 August 1958

My dear Parents,

Such a collection of letters from you that I shan't even try to be systematic in answering them.

First, thank you so much, Pa, for all your work on our behalf in relation to new cars. The Volkswagen has always looked like the best buy, but it is so ugly ... Peter has long coveted a Ford Zephyr, but this would cost half as much again. Oh well, at present our bank balance shows only the price of half a Volkswagen, so we have plenty of time to consider the choices while we try to save enough money for any kind of car. We would hope to buy one next spring, in order to have owned the car for six months before our return to Canada, and thereby avoid paying import duty.

Next, thank you, Pa, for the proofs of your articles and the cutting of no. 1. I quite like them (though less so than your articles about Canada following your visit in 1955), but we do not intend to show them to anyone in Moscow unless pressed, as we are not anxious to remind the Russians of our connection with the author. No. 2 in particular made us a little uneasy, and I would especially dislike the Embassy servants to learn about this one. The British, of course, will have seen the articles anyway, as their Embassy subscribes to the *Daily Telegraph*.

I am so sorry about the David F. situation; people do behave in the most unexpected ways, don't they? What a pity that this sour note should come to spoil an otherwise successful trip. Before you arrived in Moscow, David seemed eager to see you and to help you, and said kind and gracious things about you and what benefit you were likely to derive from the visit. So it is all very odd that he should now regard you as an intruder and be resentful of your activities. After all, you are approaching the Moscow scene from very different points of view; David was and remains the *D.T.*'s unchallenged expert on Soviet and East European affairs. I hope that, to make up for this awkwardness, you get an enthusiastic response to the articles from your Readers. I imagine that a correspondence will be provoked.

You would be proud of our rosy cheeks and shining eyes following our holiday. We are making big efforts to get to bed early and keep them that way. I hope that Henry has reassured Pa about his health concerns, and that *your* holiday, when it comes, will leave you with equally r. cheeks and s. eyes. By the way, your Austrian Baedeker was most useful, and the phrase book too came in handy once or twice.

Now I must end. I hope to type a general letter before Monday. Much love to you and to Liz,

Ever, Naomi

Moscow
18 August 1958

Dear Families,

Well, about the holiday. Peter has already written to you at length about Budapest, and most rewarding it was — by far the most memorable part of our holiday. I will continue with an account of the Austrian part.

We had quite a nice hotel in Vienna, small and modern, though with this disadvantage, that our windows overlooked the streetcar track, and this, of course, was noisy. Life in Vienna was expensive, especially the eating part. Also, in spite of its reputation, we did not find Viennese cooking very good, with the exception of the famous cakes, and these are really too rich for our well-trained stomachs.

Peter was very amused to find that the Austrians really do wear their national costume, all of the time. The senior Ministers can be observed going off to their offices complete with briefcase and well-worn short leather pants held up rather optimistically by four buttons and a pair of braces (suspenders), looking like characters in a comic opera. Peter thinks the shorts are a wonderful idea, and wonders whether he dare introduce the custom to Ottawa in summertime. He himself wore shorts (cotton, not leather) almost every day of our holiday, and a white open-necked shirt with rolled-up sleeves, and for once he was perfectly comfortable in the heat.

Perhaps the nicest thing about our holiday was the anonymity of it. We had supper one night with an Embassy colleague, and we kept in touch with the Embassy so far as our changes of address were concerned, but apart from this we were completely on our own, knew no one, and no one knew anything about us; a very welcome change from the Moscow situation.

We did a certain amount of exploring in Vienna, though many of the places that had been recommended to us, such as wine cellars where we might hear zither music, a Yugoslav restaurant with a famed gipsy fiddler, and the like, were closed for the month, "geschlossen wegen Urlaubs."

Isn't it just like the charming, feckless Austrians to close up shop "on account of holidays" just as the tourist trade arrives? We did, however, go on a *Weinprobe* in Grinzing, just outside Vienna, and enjoyed hearing the natives singing their folk songs.

I went to the hairdresser twice in one week (this costs almost nothing) and bought myself two fine dresses, both of them "sacks," each costing under twenty dollars. I gather this style is already out of fashion (hence, no doubt, the sale prices), but luckily the Moscow ladies of the Diplomatic Corps are usually six months out of date, so I should be able to wear the dresses without too much embarrassment.

The Vienna streets we found very attractive (though the women look drab compared with the stunning Hungarian women — amazing, isn't it?). And the joy of being able to sit in a coffee bar in the open air, without being stared at, and to watch the world go by, is more intense than I would ever have guessed.

As well as walking in the town, we made one pleasant excursion in the country outside Vienna, where we looked at the four houses in which Beethoven had lived in that little village, and at one point heard one of his early piano sonatas come tinkling out of a window, played by some child's hand.

By Friday (we had arrived on Monday) we felt ready to leave the city — it was becoming increasingly hot — and we set out by train for Altmuenster am Traunsee, for the only hotel in this part of Austria in which the travel agent could find us a room. The hotel was not good, though the women who ran it were very pleasant and anxious to please, even if thoroughly inefficient. The food was indifferent, but we got a good packed lunch every day to take out with us, and I guess that for three dollars a day all included we could hardly expect more. But the real snag, something the travel agent had omitted to tell us, was the location. The hotel looked onto a particularly beautiful lake and mountain range, but between the hotel and the lake, immediately under the window, lay the main road, which circled the lake, and at the side of the hotel lay the main road into the village, and there was plenty of traffic, especially motorbikes, on both roads. Fortunately, we were able to spend all day outside; the weather by this time was cooler but still sunny, in fact just right for walking. We took sleeping pills at night and managed to ignore the traffic on the whole.

We took some lovely mountain walks, and also enjoyed pleasant rural evenings, some spent in nearby Gmunden, a most attractive town of fifteenth-, sixteenth-, and seventeenth-century buildings, and others in our own village. One night there was a "band concert" by the lake, and afterwards we were lucky enough to find ourselves in the same village pub as the bandsmen, who were local village people. They continued to play and to sing for their own and for the other customers' amusement, including some lovely solo pieces played on the clarinet by a young peasant. They all drank huge quantities of beer. The tradition seems to be to order an immense tankard and pass it from hand to hand (or mouth to mouth) at the table. There is plainly a complex ritual attached, which includes a musical toast to the beer before the first gulp is taken. Peter enjoyed all this tremendously.

Another day, we had booked to go on a round trip by private bus to Salzburg and to spend the day there on our own. However, there were too few passengers to justify hire of the bus, so we went, just five passengers, in a car driven not by the bus owner but by his young assistant. Though the drive was through some stunning countryside, we were much too alarmed by the young pup's wild driving to enjoy it. Once in Salzburg we spent a pleasant day and I think saw all the important sights.

On Thursday it poured with rain all day, which didn't matter to us as we were travelling back to Vienna through most of it, but it made us realize how lucky we had been; if it had rained during our stay in Altmuenster am Traunsee we would not have such good memories of the place.

As soon as we got to Vienna the weather was fine again. We had sent a telegram two days earlier to our Vienna hotel, but apparently this was too late for them to reserve us a room. So they arranged for us to go instead to a huge old hotel on the Ring, the Hotel de France, where we had a simply mammoth room. We found the hotel staff here particularly courteous.

The next day was our last. We each went on our separate shopping expedition but met for lunch. Peter had put in an agreeable morning and had bought all he wanted. But I had been smitten with shopper's nerves (it is so important to get all one is going to need while on one's brief sorties from Moscow), and after visiting a dozen shops I had bought *nothing*, but had given myself a blinding headache and could eat no lunch! However, Peter cheered me up and fed me aspirins, and after leaving him I managed to buy a permanently pleated drip-dry skirt and a cotton jacket and a white cardigan and a hat. With our remaining few schillings we bought a dozen bananas to take back with us to offer to our most favoured friends.

All the next day was spent in travel, and now it is bag-closing time and I must stop.

Much love to both families,
Naomi.

Moscow
23 August 1958

My dear Parents and Liz,

Many happy returns of the day, Liz! I enclose a cheque with which I invite you to buy yourself a present, or, if you prefer, you can save it for future commissions on our behalf and instead choose yourself a present in Moscow.

I hope that we will hear on Tuesday that you have your visa and that all is in order for your trip. What day does the boat arrive in Leningrad?

We received another parcel of books from London yesterday, and thank you for these. We now have a really inviting library, from which people come to borrow for their pleasure reading. Last night I started on the latest K. Amis novel, but so far find it disappointing. What a pity, when his first novel was such fun (*Lucky Jim*).

Peter and Marshall took an afternoon off last week and we all four went to the Pushkin Museum to see the exhibition of looted German treasures, which are about to be returned to the Germans of East Germany. There are three lithographs by Muirhead Bone among others of the *Angliskaya Shkola*. I must write and tell Stephen. We also lined up to see the Gruesome Twosome in their shrine; all very solemn and quite impressive.

We have been socially active of late, helping our Ambassador to entertain visiting Canadian worthies and also going to parties given by others. At one black tie dinner I found myself in a slightly unnerving situation. On my left was an aging French diplomat, a military attaché, I think, and beyond him, on his left, a German diplomat, a man we know quite well. The Frenchman addressed not one word to me during the first fifteen minutes of the dinner. This did not bother me particularly, though of course it was discourteous and contrary to protocol. As it happened, I could overhear enough of his conversation with the German to be aware that they were swapping war stories. The German was boasting of his experiences on the eastern front (this is considered fair game in the present political climate), but suddenly he forgot himself and exclaimed: " ... and then we turned toward the West." At this, the Frenchman made a 45-degree turn in his chair, so that he had his back to the German and was practically nose to nose with me. "Et, alors, Madame?" he roared. This I interpreted to mean "Well, what can *you* talk about?" Not surprisingly, I was incapable of providing a sparkling conversational response. I suppose I must have babbled something, but it didn't really matter what I said, for it was clear that he had made use of me only in order to snub the German. After dinner our German acquaintance apologized to me for what had happened; I think he was pretty ashamed of his gaffe and was hoping I would not publicize it. (I didn't.)

At a different party this week some of the more junior officers from the British Embassy commented to me on Pa's articles. They felt pleased that at last the British public was going to get an idea of what Western diplomats have to face in the Soviet Union. They say it is the first time anything of the sort has appeared. We don't yet know what Sir Patrick thinks about the articles; these were personal opinions, not official comment.

Yesterday we gave a lunch for ten people, of whom three had to be invited at the last minute, as the principal guest (a Canadian astronomer) could not come, and neither could two other guests. However, it was a pleasant affair. Our lunches are much less painful events than are our dinners; I think we will concentrate mainly on this type of entertainment in future. At least they take place during office hours and we are not preventing our guests from staying home in the evening and reading a good book, or perhaps going to the ballet. While Nina and I were preparing this lunch I was able to teach her a culinary trick (unusual, as she is more experienced than I). I showed her how to peel tomatoes easily by dipping them first briefly in boiling water. She was enchanted and exclaimed "*Kak chulki!*" (Like stockings).

No more news to relate. Happy birthday, again, Liz; we will drink a toast to you this evening before we go out.

Much love,

N.

━━ ╶╴

Moscow

1 September 1958

My dear Ma and Pa,

Are you really leaving for your holiday next Wednesday? General Avidar suggested Israel as a good place for you to visit, and Peter thought this a splendid idea. But I suppose you have all your travel plans made by now. I suggest England as one of the finest countries in which to spend a holiday, especially in September, and much less trouble than going abroad. (By the way, I am liking the K. Amis book better as I read further, and I am learning a lot about Portugal from it.) The Avidars both said polite things about Mrs A.'s visit to 10 Eton Road. We like them very much. Unfortunately they will leave Moscow in October, presumably for ever.

At the British Embassy last week several people told me that they had read Pa's articles with interest. Both P. and I asked the Ambassador (British) what his opinion was concerning the articles, and he said, rather guardedly, that there was nothing with which he would disagree. This I take to be the official line, which would seem to mean that you had stepped on no Foreign Office toes. Oh, and I did not say in my earlier letter that I *didn't* like the articles; I said that I *quite* liked them. On a second reading I liked them more. Sorry if my cautious comment caused offence.

Did your photo of the whitewashed statue in Gorki Park come out? We have some successful slides of the day we all spent at Zagorsk and Pereslavl.

Lots of love to you both,

Naomi

P.S. from Peter: No objection at all if you like to show my Budapest thing to Mr Martin Moore. Obviously no attributions to be made should he use any of it.

P.

Moscow
8 September 1958

My dear Parents

I stupidly arranged a welcome-to-Moscow lunch for the Yaldens for today, and consequently have left myself no time for letter-writing. But guests have all gone now, and I just have time to dash off a line to you before the bag leaves.

We still do not know if Liz is really coming to stay, and I am in a great state of uncertainty what to do. On Friday (12th September) P. and I expect to set off on what should be a fascinating trip in the Ukraine, in some rural backwoods, the purpose being for him to identify people who ought to be in receipt of Canadian pensions from the First World War and are currently receiving nothing from Canada. He will be interviewing them in their homes. Snag is that we do not expect to be back until the 21st, and Liz, if she comes, is due on the 19th. I may desert Peter if there is a plane flying from wherever we are. Or possibly Max may be able to join him at this point. Alternatively, I may leave Liz in Janice's care, though of course Janice herself is very new and doubtless nervous. All most problematical. Well, you will hear what happened in my next. We will also be sending you open-mail letters from deepest Ukraine.

The Yaldens are a good addition to the Embassy staff, and we will enjoy their company. They, we, and the Crowes all spent a pleasant evening at the Aragvy Restaurant, Moscow's best, a Georgian place, much better than the old Astoria, if you can believe this possible.

Thanks for your last letters. Have a very good holiday.

Much love from us both,

Nao.

❦

Moscow
14 September 1958

My dear Ma and Pa

This should be written from the heart of the Ukraine, but it isn't. Peter's long-planned trip to visit the first of the Canadian First World War pensioners or their widows had finally been accepted by the Foreign Ministry, and we were to set out in one of the Embassy station wagons on Friday morning. On Thursday afternoon as I was packing our emergency food and medical supplies word came through from the Ministry that "for reasons of a temporary nature" the only road out of Moscow in the right direction was barred to us for an indefinite period. In addition, various stages of the trip were forbidden on a permanent basis, if Peter were travelling by car. Peter still intends to make what part of the journey he can as soon as the temporary ban is lifted, but I am afraid I may no longer be a part of the trip, as Liz will be here very soon. If we were disappointed, just think how the intended beneficiaries of the pension will feel when the man who has promised them 1000 roubles a month after he has identified them does not turn up. Even if Liz is staying with us Peter will leave as soon as he can, for before long the snow will be here and travel will become even more disagreeable. But it will be a pity for him to miss some of her visit. All the Foreign Ministry's fault.

A second man from the British Embassy told Peter that he liked Pa's articles. Personally, I liked them much better on a second reading — perhaps when it seemed unlikely that we were going to be thrown out immediately on the strength of them, an eventuality that we did slightly fear when we chanced upon no. 2 in Salzburg.

The Yaldens are settling in and are going to be a great asset to the Embassy. My own life is incomparably better now than it was in the early months, when I had to do all my exploring alone and without knowing any Russian. I think Janice will be a fine companion and perhaps we will even do some trips together, come the summer. At the moment the weather is cold and uninviting and the central heating is not functioning yet. Brr. (I expect you remember that our heating comes from some central source controlled by the city.) I hope the south of France is still warm and sunny and that you like your hotel.

We have given a couple of lunches for the Yaldens and have also been out ourselves to a good many parties, in fact an evening at home is so unusual that we hardly know how to settle down when we have one.

Ma, I used a recipe from one of your cookbooks, a "tutti-frutti" fruit salad, made from a bottle of rum and all kinds of soft fruit as they came into season. I had about ten quarts by the end of the summer, and hoped to be able to use the dish throughout the winter, but I am afraid the mixture has begun to ferment, so I have to start using it at once. It has already seen me through four parties, and has I think been popular.

Thanks so much for *Doctor Zhivago*, which I have already begun. A big improvement on *Not by Bread Alone*.

My fingers are frozen and there is no special news so I will stop. I hope you got my last letter, addressed to Menton. Have a happy, restful holiday.

Much love,
Naomi

—◦—

Moscow
22 September 1958

My dear Parents,

I've just read Liz's letter to you and am still laughing over her spelling of Marshall Crowe's name (Martial).

Liz arrived very tanned and healthy-looking, and fortunately the good weather she enjoyed on the voyage has accompanied her to Moscow — a surprise, as I had thought that winter was already upon us.

More frustrations concerning the Ukraine trip, but in spite of some additional obstacles that the Ministry has put in their way, Peter and Marshall set out to do what they could in a five-day much truncated version of the original trip. They left very early on Saturday morning and expect to be back on Wednesday. Meanwhile, it is rather convenient to have the daily-breader away, so that the tourists can arrange their timetable without having to take the master into consideration.

May we see a copy of Ma's "piece"? I hope she will still try to do her talk on BBC *Woman's Hour*. The Roberts parents send congratulations on Pa's articles; Ant Mud forwarded copies to them.

No time for more now. Did you get my last two letters addressed to Menton?

Much love, and have a good time,
Nao.

P.S. Thank you so much for all kinds of art books for us and for George. I haven't yet given his books to George, but I should think he will be thrilled. I will send you a cheque for the one on African art.

❦

Moscow
28 September 1958

Dear Lethbridge Family,
Dear London Family,

I have been busy introducing Liz to Moscow and vice versa since I last wrote. I have trotted her round the streets and shops (she thinks everything is outrageously expensive) and we had a good excursion yesterday around the Lenin Library, which is immense and rather attractive. She has also been included in several parties to which we were invited, especially a number of all-Canadian ones given in honour of Louise O'Connor, our Registry Clerk, who left on Saturday, to the regret of all. (She is known fondly as Louise Okohhop, which is how her name appears in Cyrillic script.)

We gave a big and very merry cocktail party for Louise ourselves after work on Friday, but immediately after this Peter retired to bed and is spending the weekend there. He came back from his trip feeling rather worn, and by Friday had developed a bass baritone voice and a stuffed-up nose. He felt wretched all yesterday but is a little perkier today and may decide to get up tomorrow. Meanwhile we have sent Liz off with some of the Canadians to see Zagorsk (the Monastery), and I have tickets for this evening for the puppet show that we saw and loved last year. Poor Peter will miss the performance this time. Another ticket for the show that I had bought is also going begging: I had ordered a ticket for Mr Singleton, Howard's father, who we think is now in Moscow, but he has not called us yet.

Peter's and Marshall's trip was moderately successful, though they managed to see only one pensioner. Perhaps they will make another attempt later.

There is really no more news of a general nature, so I will remove the carbon paper and continue on each sheet in answer to your individual letters.

* * *

So sorry to see Stephen Bone's obituary notice in the *N.Y. Herald Tribune* last week. What a sad thing. I expect you both will miss him dreadfully; he has been a friend for such a long time.

George was delighted with one of the Chagall books, especially when he found in it a reproduction of the black-and-white painting of a Jew that he owns (he had once sent Chagall a photo of the original). The other book he thinks he already has and is checking. May we keep it if he does not want it, or should we send it back? On the very day that I gave him the books he had received a letter from Chagall, so he was very happy. I gave him the Braque book too, but am keeping the African book until Christmas. Perhaps we will eventually give him all the other books as well, but not all at once.

I think Liz is having quite a good time. It was nice for me to have her company while Peter was away. We are trying to persuade her to stay until Friday or Saturday and to go home by air. I think she is too late anyway to obtain the appropriate visas in order to travel by train, as she had considered doing. Tomorrow I hope to take her to the GUM fashion show, which you and I never did get to see, Ma.

I hope you had a restful holiday. Did you get my letters? I have had one letter and one postcard from you.

Much love,
Naomi.

Moscow
5 October 1958

My dear Parents,

I saw Liz off on the TU–104 in beautiful weather yesterday. Today it is warm but grey and sunless, and the unmitigated gloom of the Moscow streets has driven me to draw the curtains earlier than necessary. We went out for a walk to cheer ourselves up, but it had the opposite effect. No wonder Chekhov's characters are so despairing — though there was more gaiety in his day than is to be found now. Incidentally, I am enthralled by *Doctor Zhivago*, though I feel a little anxious as regards the likely fate of its author.

I think we gave Liz a good time; I hope she feels the same way about her holiday. Anyway, it was fun having her here, and I shall be a bit bleak next week. Please thank her for her telegram, which came this morning.

I am having "Tee" (as my invitation card puts it) with Madame Avidar next week. She intends to call you during the week that they will spend in England en route to Israel at the end of the month.

No special news. Peter continues to cough but is improving. I hope that you are both well.

With love,
Ever,
Nao.

Moscow
6 October 1958

My dear Ma, Pa and Liz,

Peter's father died peacefully yesterday. We heard this morning. I don't know the cause of death — perhaps a cerebral hemorrhage. We will phone them tonight.

Affectionately,
Naomi

Moscow
13 October 1958

My dear Parents,

Thank you for your telegram sent to Peter. He was very shattered by the news, poor thing, and is still feeling pretty blue most of the time, though it helped a lot when he finally managed to get through to Lethbridge by phone on Tuesday evening. (He tried again and again on Monday, but there was no answer, and he felt desperate.) He phoned again at 8:00 a.m. Thursday, which was 10:00 p.m. Wednesday in Lethbridge, after the funeral had taken place. So far as Peter can tell from their voices, Mary and his mother are very calm, though no doubt they make a big effort to control their emotions when talking to him.

Of course we considered having Peter fly out to Lethbridge, but five days compassionate leave is all that is allowed, and the fares would amount to more than we *have*, let alone what we can afford. So, since they seemed to be in control of the situation, we decided instead to try to bring Mother Roberts over to England for a holiday next summer. We have already suggested the idea to her, but I anticipate that we will have a hard job persuading her. If she should come, Peter would take his leave at the same time and would drive her around England and take her to visit the few remaining Roberts relatives. Unfortunately, I know that we will never get her to agree to *stay* with anyone (as a guest), unless she can bring herself to overcome her life-long principles. Well, I'm sure the trip can be managed from our point of view, if only we can persuade her to accept.

The cause of death was a cerebral hemorrhage, like the Pope's but quicker. Father Roberts had been unwell for the past three or four weeks suffering from "hypertension," but I don't think this would have brought on the stroke, though it might have lessened his ability to recover from it. I am only guessing at this — it will be another week before we can expect a letter.

Poor Roberts family: they will miss him dreadfully. I am so glad he lived long enough to see Mary move to a job that at last promised to please her, and in Lethbridge too, so that she was already living at home and there need be no upheaval. (She moved to Lethbridge about the middle of September.) She and her mother will be able to keep one another company.

No news from Moscow; we cancelled all our social engagements for two weeks, except for one next Thursday when we are invited to the Yugoslavs, which is too unusual an occasion to be missed. Oh, yes, I should add that I went to a small farewell tea party given by Mrs Avidar.

My own health has suddenly become much better during the last few weeks. I don't know if this is due to the mild autumn weather, which always seems to suit me, but for once I actually have energy to spare and a certain amount of enthusiasm to go with it. Until this happened, I hadn't realized how weary and listless I feel at other times. I hope your respective holidays have put you all in the same welcome state.

Ma, when you are out shopping downtown, would you look out for new cotton work-dresses for Nina, please? Perfectly standard, button-down front with white collar and cuffs. Colour preference: one pink and one blue (but any other pretty colour acceptable) and *lightweight* for summer. They should not be expensive, for I am already giving her a new overcoat in lieu of the rest of her uniform. Size 42 hips — she insists that her working clothes be roomy enough for two Ninas. I should think that Thomas Wallis might be a good place to try. No hurry about this at all.

I have finished reading *Doctor Zhivago* and am most enthusiastic about it. It is hard to put down as it sweeps along over the years and over the country.

George did already have a copy of the second Chagall book, so may we keep it, please?

Much love,

Nao.

───

Moscow

18 October 1958

My dear Pa, Ma, and Liz,

Your letters were very genuine and gave me a lot of comfort. And thank you too for sending a telegram to me and one to my Mother. She will appreciate it as much as I did.

It's still not very real, nor will it be, I think, until I go home and find him missing. I suppose you can't say that the death of a man of seventy-two years is totally unexpected, but his was unexpected in that no one, including the doctors, took seriously the minor ailment that had kept him in bed a few days, and that, so I gather from my telephone conversations with Lethbridge, culminated in a stroke.

I still haven't heard by post from my Mother, although he died two weeks ago today, and it wasn't very nice to have a letter from her last Monday, written four days before he died, saying that he was much better, had been out in the garden, and would be up again soon. She sounded very cheerful.

It's a crowning mercy that Mary chose that particular time to settle in Lethbridge again. She actually moved in permanently less than a week before it happened.

I'm phoning them again tomorrow morning. When letters are two weeks and more en route, writing is almost futile.

Many thanks for your sympathy and kindness, and love to you all.

Peter

⚬

Moscow
19 October 1958

My dear Parents and Liz,

Thank you so much for all your letters to Peter, which he greatly appreciated. Toward the end of last week he began to perk up a bit, and now seems in a much more serene state. He has phoned his Mother three times since his Father died, and once — luckily — just before, so that although he did not speak to his Father at the time, at least the old man would have felt in close touch with Peter. Postal communication between us is horribly slow.

On a lighter note: the great excitement of last week was the appearance, for one day only, of BANANAS! Queer, stunted little things, hardly bigger than a large carrot, but with the familiar taste. I bought five kilos, most of which I gave away, but we still enjoyed an orgy at home. I also made two banana-bread loaves, and froze one against a banana-less day.

While I was standing in line at the outdoor vendor's kiosk I rashly allowed myself to become engaged in a discussion. One of the good citizens (a woman) remarked: "I wonder where these bananas come from?" The inevitable Mr Know-it-All responded, "They come from Africa. Look at the African writing on the box." Sure enough, there were words in a non-Cyrillic script on the packing-cases, but the words were "*Diesa sidda uppa*" (or something of the sort, presumably meaning "This side up"). Timidly (pedantically?) I offered, "I think it is written in a Scandinavian language." Mr Know-it-All gave me a withering look, turned his back on me and announced, "All bananas come from Africa." Needless to say, I did not attempt to pursue the subject, and no one else was so reckless as to question the statement. Well, it passed the time while we waited our turn.

Liz, you did me a good turn. You started us off drinking tea instead of coffee for breakfast, and Peter actually seems to prefer it. As it is cheaper, easier to prepare, and better for us, I am delighted. I also drink three cups each morning, instead of my one cup of coffee, and the extra intake must surely be good for me. (Goodness, I sound like Montaigne writing essays about the intimate details of his daily life.)

The Crowes will be staying in a hotel while in London, arriving I think on 10 November. I asked Doris how she felt about parties and she said that she would love to come to dinner with you, and would be equally happy to see just the family or to be there with other guests. A cocktail party, however, or any stand-up party, is out of the question for her, though I suppose not for Marshall. I expect that Liz has told you that Doris is pregnant and that her legs swell up and ache. Doris must have mixed feelings about this turn of events, for she has painful memories of giving birth to a baby that did not survive during their previous Moscow posting. Presumably the family will make arrangements for an *accouchement* outside the Soviet Union this time. Doris was brave to agree to a second Moscow posting, I feel, given her nightmare experience. (I know only a little about the circumstances.)

Peter copied the attached list of titles from the Autumn Books section of *The Spectator*. If these books come your way, Pa, would you bear him in mind? We were very pleased with the load you sent us via Liz. How did you like the picture George sent you by hand of Liz?

No special news. I hope to hear about the parents' holiday tomorrow.

Much love,

N.

Moscow

27 October 1958

My dear Parents and Liz,

Alas, all we received last week was the P.S. to a non-existent letter from Ma. Perhaps all will be righted on Tuesday. I hope there will be some message for George, as he was inquiring wistfully whether I had not yet heard from my sister?

Peter was Chargé d'Affaires *ad interim* from Wednesday to Sunday last week, and quite enjoyed his fling, though he was even busier than usual. He had to go once to the airport to see off the Arab Vice-President and once to the train station to meet Gomulka, and once to a Kremlin reception, also for the Arab V.P. Marshall was in Helsinki, a place he greatly enjoyed.

Lois Marshall, the revered Canadian soprano, gave her second concert in Moscow on Tuesday, and the Chargé and I escorted her from the concert hall to the Crowes' home afterwards. A whole lot of Russian musicians had been invited to Doris's party for the distinguished guest, but inevitably all were "called out of town" at the last moment, though some of them may in fact have been at the concert. It seemed at one point that the musicians actually would come, and Doris wonders whether the award of the Nobel Prize for Literature to Pasternak was the reason that they were after all prevented from attending. You will have heard of the virulent attacks on Pasternak that appeared in the Soviet press on Saturday and Sunday. (Nothing appeared on Thursday and Friday.) No matter what they did, the Russians were bound to look a bit foolish, but this response seems to me more likely to harm their cause both at home and abroad than any other stand they could have taken. Especially as, so I have heard, unbound copies of *Dr. Z.* in Russian are circulating among the Russians (but don't make use of this information, please). Anyone who reads the book must see how wild the accusations are, and with what humanity the Russian people are portrayed.

Peter's spirits improve week by week, but I wish I could get him out on holiday soon. However, I doubt that he will get out before next summer, unfortunately.

There is no more special news just now. I hope to have your letters to answer next time. So, till next week,

Much love,

N.

—◦—

Moscow

2 November 1958

My dear Ma and Pa,

You have written such kind letters to me lately; I hope you'll forgive my not replying sooner (bar a short note). Truth is, there's been no time this week for writing letters, or even for calling one's soul one's own: since Monday six dinners, two lunches, and four cocktails. I call it no fun at all, and by the time you've heard the twentieth person tell all about Pasternak, the same "all" as you heard last night, you begin to weary even of that fascinating subject.

Our main preoccupation just now is a telegram from my Mother announcing, to my complete astonishment, that she will be delighted to spend the month of June in England with me. Considering that she has never been abroad, except into the northern fringes of the United States, and hasn't even been in Eastern Canada for thirty years, a trip to England will be a large adventure for her, and one that I believe she will enjoy.

Our plan in light of this is to come to England about the first of June (supposing that the Posol will give me leave — he's due back from Canada tomorrow), picking up a Volkswagen in Germany on the way. I'd prefer to buy British, but there isn't anything British for that kind of money. We'll spend the month of June in London and touring elsewhere in Britain.

If the invitation still holds, I should like to take seriously your offer to put us up when we are in London — which certainly won't be all the time. This would be far more pleasant for us and for my Mother than staying in a hotel; it would also, if I may say so, be cheaper, and this is a consideration. Pa's characteristically generous offer to help out with cash is kind and generous. But I think we'll manage. Mary, I'm sorry to say, won't be coming, at least I assume not. She has just started the first job she has ever had that gives her some real satisfaction, and makes some serious demands on her knowledge and experience, and she certainly won't want to leave it, or to demand extra holidays, yet.

For some time after the news came of my Father's death, I felt very badly that I had not somehow arranged to go home. Thank God I didn't, because this is a far more sensible and practical way of spending the money — rather less money, too. It gives my Mother something to plan for and to look forward to during what will be the most difficult months, and it will give her a lot of satisfaction to see the remaining family — really only Maud in Newcastle — and to visit places that she has heard about almost daily for forty years. I remember that my first visit to Kingswood School in Bath, which I had heard my Father talk about all my life, was an almost mystic experience. Not that I want my Mother's time in England to be a melancholy pilgrimage around the *pamyatniky*, but that will be a big part of the interest for her. She's not given to melancholy anyway.

You have no doubt been following the Pasternak affair. It beats all, and the most astounding document came in *Pravda* this morning, Pasternak's letter to Khrushchev. I have just finished translating it; perhaps you would like to read it.

Dear Nikita Sergeyevich,

I am appealing to you personally, to the Central Committee of the Communist Party and to the Soviet Government.

From the report of Comrade Semichastny I have learned that the government "will put no obstacles in the way of my departure from the USSR."

For me this is impossible. I am tied to Russia by birth, by life, and by my work.

I cannot conceive of my fate separately or outside hers. Whatever may have been my mistakes and delusions, I did not imagine that I would become the centre of a political campaign such as has blown up around my name in the West.

Realizing this, I have informed the Swedish Academy of my voluntary refusal of the Nobel Prize.

Departure beyond the borders of my country is the same for me as death, and I therefore ask you not to take these extreme measures with me.

Laying my hand on my heart, I say that I have done something for Soviet literature, and I can still be of use to it.

B. PASTERNAK   31 October, 1958.

The thought of Pasternak grovelling before Khrushchev is so repulsive that one hates to read of it. At the same time the letter grovels as little as possible in the circumstances, doesn't unequivocally admit any mistakes, and has tremendous dignity. Presumably its publication means that they will let him stay in the country. Max Frankel, who had a couple of interviews with him, thinks he will be allowed to keep his dacha and won't be otherwise bothered. The Russians have come out of it very badly, both at home and abroad, and there's comfort in that.

I'm intending to write to Lizzie as well by this bag, but if I don't manage to do it, please give her my love, and Na's.

Our love to you both, P.

Moscow
3 November 1958

Dear Ma, Pa, and Liz

Thank you for all your letters last week, but oh dear, the missing one from Ma of the week before has not turned up, and George keeps asking me if I haven't heard from my sister, meaning : 1) What about the Picasso book? and 2) Didn't your parents like the Zverev pictures I sent them?

The latest on the Crowe front is that Marshall has applied for home leave for the whole family from March to May, or is it February to April, I forget. I hope the leave is granted.

One morning last week when it was cold but sunny I offered to take the two older Crowe girls for a walk along the boulevards. The little girls wore their brightly coloured Canadian winter jackets. Unexpectedly, we were approached by a man who spoke to me directly, a rare occurrence. I thought he was admiring the little girls, and I said something like "Yes, aren't they sweet?" But he replied (so far as I could make out), "Never mind the children, how much do you want for the coats?" I stammered that they were not my own children and we hurried off in some alarm. Wasn't he the bold one to make such a proposal in a public place? But perhaps it was just another case of attempted entrapment. (Of course foreigners are not permitted to make private sales to Soviet citizens.)

To return to your letters: many thanks for Pa's offers of financial assistance. We can just manage Mother R's fare, but if we can persuade her to overcome her scruples and spend her nights in London under your roof, that will be a big help to us.

No, don't bother to try to buy the books that Peter marked as interesting, and especially please don't buy Proust in fourteen volumes in any language! I don't mean to countermand his requests, but we are trying hard to save a few dollars each month, and we already have more books than we have space to accommodate them. If he is really keen I expect he will ask again, but meanwhile please do nothing. I think the books advertised in the *TLS* appealed to him on the basis that you might have copies at home — I will ask him. Liz, you aren't forgetting the books I asked you to obtain as Christmas presents for Tommy Crowe and for Lilya, are you? Your letter was very good and funny.

Peter has told you about our social week, which was almost unprecedented in its load of parties. This one will be quieter, I hope.

I am going to write a separate letter to Ma.

Much love,

N.

— ⁓ —

Moscow
4 November 1958

My dear Ma,

I return your manuscript with some comments, some of them mine and some Peter's. I hope he will find time to add to this letter the answer to your inquiries about trades, etc.

My general comment is that you should be either *more* serious about the misery of Russian life, or else much *less* serious, and in any case more sympathetic. I think if you were going to write more seriously you should be armed with more expert knowledge, and that for you it would be best to treat the subject rather lightly. Possibly we who live here and read and talk so much about Russian life are super-sensitive and super-critical, so don't be offended by my comments. All the same, I would revise the article, taking as your guide your last sentence about the errand-boy, which expresses exactly what is lacking here, and is the best idea in the whole article. There are lots of other good passages, too, but I feel that you could improve the whole, and give it more unity. You rather wander between "How the Russians live" and "How a tourist (or foreigner) is treated in Russia," two very different subjects.

Sorry to be so harsh in my comments. Don't be discouraged. (I thought if I was going to comment at all, it was best to be frank.)

Much love,

N.

P.S. Briefly: People can go to a variety of schools of the "Texnikum" type if they can pass the entrance exam and have completed seven years of general education; these schools *may* be full-time, but more often students attend night classes or off-shift classes. When qualified, they may be conscripted into labour where they are most needed, not necessarily a place of their own choice.

Moscow

10 November 1958

My dear Parents and Liz,

I can see this is going to be a hard week. We have four dinner parties (one of them here) and two lunches (one here). But more important, our team of Inspectors from Ottawa has just arrived and the place will be a madhouse till they leave.

It is a pretty critical visit for all of us here from a personal point of view, as Ottawa threatens to do away with the system of subsidized roubles and not to make up the difference — or anything like it — by adding to the dollars paid into our living allowances account. So each member of the Embassy staff has written out a monthly budget, and the officers find (not really to their surprise) that far from saving wads of money they actually pay for the privilege of serving here. I found that we go in the hole at the rate of one hundred dollars a month; no wonder our bank balance always seems so low. If I had not been earning a salary in Ottawa last year, thus providing us with some savings to draw upon, we could not have managed. Before leaving Ottawa we had to take a thousand dollar posting loan from the Government (admittedly at a low rate of interest) in order to go and serve that same Government abroad! (We are by no means alone in this situation; the Yaldens took a two thousand dollar loan.)

All this study of our finances has persuaded Peter that we may justifiably entertain less often and less elaborately, which is what I have wanted all along, so that is good. Trouble is, one's hospitality debts do mount up, and we would be ashamed to feed our former hosts baked beans when they had served us a four-course banquet.

The Inspectors were due to arrive at 6:30 yesterday, and I volunteered to feed them, and the Ambassador too if he cared to come at the last minute, which, as you remember, is the only kind of invitation from his staff that doesn't throw him into a panic. Of course we were Nina-less, as it was Sunday, so I cooked all afternoon and laid the table, and behaved just like a non-Foreign Service wife, and then Pete and the Ambassador returned from the airport to tell me that the Inspectors had decided to come (from Warsaw) on a later plane. However, Posol accepted to eat with us after all, and it was a successful occasion. He has returned in good form from his holiday (although much of it was spent in hospital, first because of a nose operation and later because of flu), and as we were all hungry we consumed most of the Inspectors' share as well as our own. I felt my stock with Posol rising as he ate (it has always been pretty low), so in the end the Inspectors did me a good turn, except that now I have to arrange another party for them.

By the way, Ma, Janice taught me a good trick: she serves chopped, blanched almonds sautéd in oil on top of vegetables, and it does seem to lift canned peas and beans into the party class. This supper for six (if the three Inspectors had come) was to have been a test case. I wanted to see whether it was possible to serve a sit-down dinner in our flat without a maid, and yet not have to embarrass everyone by running around with plates and dishes in a *neculturno* manner. I think it could be done, with careful planning, and if we lose our subsidized roubles we may decide to do without any servant at all. At present we pay Nina about fifty to sixty dollars a month, counting her social insurance and perks of all kinds, but this would go up to about a hundred and thirty dollars a month according to the threatened new rate, and we feel we can't afford as much. Well, enough of our financial woes — sorry that this was so boring and self-centred.

Posol has agreed to let Peter have leave in June (did we tell you that P.'s mother had cabled that she *would* come on our proposed trip?), so please arrange not to be away at that time. It is nice for us to have this treat to look forward to, six months hence.

Ma, your letter of 15th October arrived by the *sea-bag* at the end of last week. But it was full of interesting stories, even if nearly a month old. I have felt remorseful about my harsh comments on your new article. If they paid you fifteen guineas for the first one, I am plainly not a good judge, and should shut up. Congratulations — that is much more than the *D.T.* ever paid me for my bits and pieces from Canada. But I still feel that you should distinguish in your longer article between "How the Russians live" and "What a tourist should expect" — also, come to that, "How foreign residents live."

I have managed to do a little more reading than usual in the last weeks, and want to repeat our thanks for all the books Pa sends us. It was especially nice of him to part with his copy of *Dr. Z.* We also lend books to several friends, notably wives at the British Embassy, and I always feel happy that we are able to do so.

Isn't the Pasternak case fantastic? Surely the Soviet authorities are doing themselves grave harm in the eyes of the world and will lose many potential recruits to Communism? When Canadian performers come over here and become starry-eyed on account of the enthusiastic reception they always receive, we shall be able to remind them that not every worthy artist in the S.U. enjoys similar acclaim.

I had yet another letter from Lady Pentland after her tea with Ma, and she kindly sent me some more magazines. I found her good company, didn't you, Ma? Her daughter is a very attractive person too.

If you own a copy of the Sally Belfrage book about her experiences in Russia and could part with it until June I would very much like to borrow it, please.

Much love, N.

Moscow
15 November 1958

My dear Parents and Liz,

Thank you, Ma, for your two letters, the magazine, and all the catalogues. I am a bit doubtful that Nina would wear an Eskimo-type headdress such as you describe. Headgear in this country is conventional, and Nina wears all winter a hat of, I think, Russian sable, much handsomer than anything I have or am likely to own. But I think she would like an ordinary wool square to wear over her shoulders under her coat, and I see many nice ones advertised. Her winter coat is grey, and the new one I have ordered for her in lieu of a new winter uniform will be (of course) blue. Incidentally, Nina was thrilled to receive the royal blue dress that was her *podarok* (gift) from me. Mother Roberts kindly administered the purchase of this garment in Lethbridge, and she did a good job.

I gave Liz a list of Bright Ideas regarding Christmas presents for Peter, and we can add to that any of the books we have mentioned recently (though for my sake *not* Proust in fourteen volumes!). Liz has got it wrong if she told you that I was hinting that I would like a *heavy* sweater, as what I really wanted was one to wear in the apartment, which is of course centrally heated. As a matter of fact my need is not so great now, as I intercepted the cardigan I was intending to give to Pratchka (the laundress) at Christmas (she will get a dress length of pretty material, instead). But what I would *really* like is a bottle of codeine tablets, only I don't want to wait till Christmas, as we are at rock bottom now. As Liz can confirm, we have sent you merely token gifts, so please don't shame us by being very generous.

Peter and I were very amused at Ma's description of your awful party. Sounds even worse than one of ours.

We had a letter from Peter's mother last week, saying that she thought she would fly direct from Lethbridge to London over the Pole, adding "Can this really be I?" She seems properly excited about it all, and I am so glad she has accepted the offer, even to the extent of being a guest in the family home. Both she and Mary are feeling very sad and lonely, and planning for the summer may provide a welcome distraction. Our latest scheme is that P. should fetch his Volkswagen from Germany (yes, it had to be a VW after all, on account of $$$) and then should drive to meet his mother in Amsterdam, where she has to change planes. But as usual, this plan may change.

It has been another hectic week, with a dinner party on five nights, and the odd cocktail party and lunch too. In addition, the presence of the Inspectors has meant that Peter often didn't come home till after seven o'clock. Thank goodness that particular visit is at an end. They were quite a sympathetic bunch, and I don't think the threatened cut in allowances will come into effect for some time, nor will it be as severe as had been suggested.

Much love to you all,

Nao.

Moscow
22 November 1958

My dear Ma, Pa, and Liz,

Thanks for long letters from Ma and Liz, and I am ready to forgive the absence of a letter from Pa if he is really reading 100 books a week, surely a demoralizing task. George could not read Ma's handwriting (what would he have made of mine or Pa's?), so I had to read aloud her letter to him.

Sorry that the BBC turned Ma down, but the *Talks to Women's Groups* sounds an interesting possibility. Uncle Willie once wrote to me that he wished I had come to Cheltenham to address his Club when I was in England; would you be interested in doing that?

As things now stand, we would not arrive in England before the 3rd or 4th of June, so that will not interfere with your plans to visit Jonathan's grave on June 1. One of these days I will be able to accompany you to Wye, and I would like to do so.

Ma, thank you so much for all the parcels. I am glad to have the book about silver marks, which I have lent to George, and I hope he returns it. The candles and the holder will look very nice on the sideboard at the next dinner party we give, if we can bring ourselves ever to give one again.

Last night we went to a really super party at the Thomases and the Seawards, in their adjoining flats, and after experiencing such a jolly evening we decided that we couldn't stand another of our dull dinners. The British Embassy officers currently in Moscow are nearly all talented party-givers; most are terrific dancers who also enjoy spontaneous music-making and singing. They are also of course bright and capable colleagues, hard-working and well informed, according to our own officers.

We were taken last week to see Ulanova dance in *Chopiniana*, followed by a scene from the *Nutcracker Suite*. Our hosts were my ex-teacher and her husband. Peter was particularly tired and cross that evening, and tactlessly replied when his host asked him how he had enjoyed the ballet, "It was wonderful. It was so short." (We were out before 10:00 instead of at 11:30 or 12:00, as is usual.) The hosts were not particularly pleased at his comment. Can't say that I blame them.

The other big excitement of the week was on Monday, when I bravely went to a cocktail party on my own, as Peter was so tired. It was probably a splendid party, but unfortunately I arrived a week late. My hostess opened the door to me wearing no make-up and no stockings, with a small child on her arm and an expression of total shock. The invitation had been by telephone only, and the message-taker must have made a mistake.

I am delighted to find that I can read a Chekhov play and understand the text fairly easily. I had no idea that I had got to the reading stage, not having tried it recently. I do very little work on my Russian, so I conclude that even an adult can absorb a foreign language if sufficiently exposed to it, though of course not nearly as fast as a child can.

No more now. We both look forward eagerly to our holiday in England, and I am especially glad that there is something bright on the horizon for Peter.

Much love,

N.

Moscow
1 December 1958

My dear Parents and Liz,

Many thanks for Liz's note and Ma's letter and all the parcels. The type-writer ribbon was just right, Liz. None of the books has come yet — perhaps tomorrow. I am most grateful to you for all your shopping. I am enclosing a cheque from Gorringes made out to me (refund for a sweater that was out of stock), and please do cash it and use it to defray some of the expenses you have incurred on my behalf.

I have ordered a parcel to be delivered to you from Fortnum and Mason, so please leave unopened until December 25 anything that arrives from F & M. It isn't very exciting, I'm afraid.

No, I don't think we will have to let Nina go after all. If they do indeed change our rouble rate it may not happen for some months. So yes, please do go ahead and buy her one of those maid's uniforms that Ma cleverly found.

Last week we were out to dinner or had guests here every night except Friday. On that day we went to the Ararat Restaurant after a cocktail party. This party was given by Sir Patrick Reilly in order to entertain fifty British student-teachers who had been in Russia for seven weeks, a fascinating and brave venture. They split up into small groups dispersed all across the Soviet Union from the Ukraine to Central Asia, and in some cases were billeted upon Russian families in their homes. One girl in particular among those I spoke to made some very intelligent and interesting observations; others were less articulate, but they may just have been stunned after their seven weeks' experience. They were certainly all very resourceful. I think they probably did a good job in representing the free world in the places where they stayed, and after seven weeks they must have carried away a pretty accurate impression of what life is like for the Russians.

Well, as I was saying, we went to the Ararat Restaurant with the Yaldens and had a fairly revolting meal in quite pleasant surroundings, to the accompaniment of a three-piece Armenian band playing strange Armenian instruments. Toward the end of our meal, a waiter came across bearing a huge black fish on a platter and offered it to us, as we thought, for sale. We declined, and he took it away. An hour later a group of three extremely handsome students from Yerevan came over to our table and the spokesman said: "I'm sorry you did not like the fish I sent you. It was a special Armenian fish, and as I saw that you are foreigners, I wanted to present it to you, as is the Armenian custom." He then marched off, very offended and slightly drunk. When we had recovered from the shock, Max dashed after the three and brought them back to our table. We then mollified them over a bottle of peculiarly nasty Armenian cognac ("12 years old"), and finally drove them in the station wagon to the Agricultural Exhibition. They claimed that they were going to skate there; or perhaps they were just going to cross the road to the Ostankino Hotel, where no doubt they were staying. It was all an unusual and interesting experience.

Most of last week Monette, the architect for the Department, was in Moscow on business, and Peter was very preoccupied with helping him dicker with the Russians about the new addition to the Embassy building that is promised. Monette is a French Canadian who has lived in France most of his life, and now has a permanent posting in Paris, from where he makes sorties to the European missions. We entertained him quite often, and had a merry time with him. He remarked to me that Peter had been very diplomatic and helpful in the dealings with the Russians, and I suggested facetiously that he repeat this comment to Monsieur Léger. "Yes, I will, I will," he said, and I think perhaps he really will.

One night we got tickets for the three of us to attend a production at the Bolshoi, where Galina Ulanova was dancing the role of Juliet. It is very hard to obtain tickets for any of Ulanova's performances, and many foreigners here — indeed, Russians too — never get a chance to see her, but it was our third opportunity to watch her dance, so we are unusually lucky. A few tickets to most cultural events are made available for purchase to each of the Embassies, and having such a small staff as we do at the Canadian Embassy works in our favour in this regard. As you undoubtedly know, Ulanova is famous for her exceptional grace; I especially admired her rippling arm movements in *Swan Lake*; she seemed to have no bones at all. There is another superb dancer whom we have also had the good fortune to see: Maya Pliesetskaya. She is, I think, the Prima Ballerina designate, and is only waiting for Ulanova to retire in order to achieve this rank. But the Russians are very loyal to their stars, and despite her age (getting on for fifty) Ulanova remains the Prima Ballerina.

It is past lunchtime and I am weak with hunger, so will write no more. Much love,

Ever,

Nao.

————

Moscow
5 December 1958
(Day of the Constitution)

My dear Ma,

What a good Ma you are to send me all those parcels. Please thank Pa for the two books for Lilya and thank Liz for the Chekhov plays in English translation, which I am delighted to have.

The black sweater is exactly what I needed, and with Janice's help I have recently finished making my Black Watch skirt and am now making a jerkin to go with it, so the sweater has arrived at just the right time. Your Christmas presents will probably come in the next bag.

The holly will be put to use very soon. I am glad to have some Christmassy decorations, as I don't intend to put up a tree this year. Last year I bought an enormously tall, skinny monster that was hard to decorate; it also shed pine needles all over the floor. After all my unrewarding work on the tree, we asked one another for whom we had put it up, and decided it must have been for Nina's benefit, and as she was in a sullen mood all over Christmas it was a rather wasted effort. So, candles and holly it shall be this year, and, if necessary, last year's Christmas cards to add to the display.

I heard from Kris recently, and she is feeling pretty unsettled in Ottawa and wishes they were back in Moscow. However, she writes merrily and comically.

We had only two dinners and two lunches this week, so our social life has been less of a strain. Three dinners and one lunch next week. I wonder why we all do this to one another.

We have invited Howard Singleton (en poste in Helsinki) to join us here for Christmas. He will stay for a week probably, and there will doubtless be lots of parties during that time, either in our home or elsewhere. In fact we already have permission to bring him to a New Year's party to which we were invited.

Much love,

Nao.

Later bulletin, 8 December:

Latest catastrophe is that one of the wings of the apartment building where the Moores used to live (you remember?) has been declared by the Russians to be unsafe, and three of our families have to evacuate. This, mark you, is a building that was put up less than two years ago; so much for Soviet construction. We anticipate that the other wings, where we also have Embassy apartments, will probably be condemned too before long. New flats have been provided elsewhere, but lots of money will have to be spent on refitting them and redecorating them before they are deemed habitable, and of course all the taxpayers' money that paid for the improvements to the old flats has now gone down the drain. The Yaldens are among those affected. We are fortunate that we did not take over the Moores' flat as we had once considered doing. Oh, Moscow! The French families who live in the condemned wing, and who put in improvements at personal expense, have so far refused to move; I wonder what will happen.

Peter is very gloomy about the Berlin crisis and thinks there is a good chance of war in May. What is your opinion? It hardly bears thinking on, does it?

Much love, again, N.

~ ~

Moscow

15 December 1958

My dear Parents and Liz,

What a heavy week we had, with a dinner party every night except Wednesday, on which night people just dropped in on us and stayed till midnight. We also had the Yaldens sleeping here on two nights, as their new apartment is almost too cold and too damp to be habitable, a most depressing situation for them. One interesting feature is that a burst water pipe has caused their dining room floor to buckle, and there is a large mound in the floor, six feet across and two feet high, the like of which I have never seen. It is really very comic to look at, but not very funny to live with.

Thank you for Pa's letter and Liz's two letters. The big box came and I have put it away unopened.

Today's family news is that *if* all goes well (and I consider it a pretty big "if") I should produce a junior Roberts on or about 28 July, which is a mighty convenient date, as I can just stay on in England following our holiday, assuming that Mr Khrushchev doesn't prevent the latter. Anyway, hoping that all goes smoothly with me and the world, the Doc says that I should ask you to ask Cousin Henry to book me a hospital bed for the end of July, so please will you?

We are giving a minute dinner party tonight, and then we will give no more parties till after Christmas, except perhaps we will invite some people for drinks in order to introduce Howard around. We had a biggish lunch here last week. Oh, how sick we are of parties!

No more now. I guess this will be the last letter you receive before Christmas, so have a happy one.

Much love, N.

P.S. I would prefer that you not spread around the news of my condition until the first four months have passed. At least don't speak of it outside the family, please.

P.P.S. Peter is wild with excitement!

◆ ～

Moscow
22 December 1958

My dear Ma, Pa and Liz,

Many thanks, Ma, for your nice long letter.

Last Monday, when we had a very small dinner party, I used the Price's candles on the table in the white holder, and they did not drip, you will be glad to know. Paola and Vero Roberti were among the guests, and Paola annoyed another female guest by claiming that it was all nonsense that foreigners were secretly followed in Moscow streets. Actually of course Paola was just being provocative for the fun of it, but the other guest got very hot under the collar.

I had tried to add some sparkle to the meal on this occasion by preparing a hollandaise sauce to serve over the all-too-familiar canned green beans. I made the sauce in the top of a double boiler and cautioned Nina that on no account should the sauce be allowed to heat to boiling point. Alas, when the dish was served the beans were covered with little gritty pieces of what looked like overcooked scrambled eggs. No one commented (neither did I), but I felt quite thrown off balance for a while. When I questioned the maids afterwards I learned that they had poured the sauce onto the beans ahead of serving time and had then put the entire dish into a 450-degree oven! That'll do it.

The next night the Robertis and two Italian bachelors gave a huge dinner and dance in the banquet room of the Metropole, complete with band. It was an enjoyable occasion, but Peter and I left soon after the dancing began, just because we had been at far too many parties in recent nights.

But on a more positive note, we attended a most interesting party last Saturday. The Embassy's former gardener, a gentle and dignified old man, a Greek by birth, who made a lot of money before the Revolution and was put in prison and labour camps to get over it, has finally got permission in his fading years to go to Greece, where he has a daughter.

His son, the local administrator at the Swedish Embassy (the equivalent of our George Costakis), gave a farewell party for Mr Apizidi in his delightful apartment, where the walls are covered in icons and interesting pictures, including several Van Wiessens and a Chagall. Marshall Crowe and John Fast were there too, also George and his wife, George's brother and *his* wife, of course old Apizidi, and his other son plus wife, the wife of young Apizidi (the host), and three stunning and well-mannered sons. The three wives and three sons are all Soviet citizens. It was a pleasant and unusual evening, and we consider ourselves fortunate to have been a part of it.

Your plans for 6 June sound terrific, Ma. No, I've never seen the Trooping of the Colour. You did not say whether you had enjoyed *My Fair Lady* — did you?

The Sally Belfrage book came, but I haven't started it yet. Peter skimmed through the book and was very sniffy at first, but later modified his judgment slightly.

Peter says that *War and Peace* was shot in Italy. I enjoyed the movie but did not feel that the characters corresponded very well to the originals, especially Pierre. Natasha was all right, and Kutyuzov. How funny that you were bored by *Where the Cranes Fly*. Most people rave about it, though I have heard the odd dissident comment. I am ashamed to say that I have not seen it.

Poor Nina came in on Wednesday in floods of tears, left for home right away, and stayed away until today. Her sister's husband, aged thirty, had suffered a sudden heart attack and had died at once, quite unexpectedly. Her sister is twenty-five and has two small children. We were driving away from the Embassy in one of the office cars on Wednesday just as Nina was leaving, and I asked the driver to stop and offer her a lift, which she refused. He returned to the car and commented that Nina was crying. I said yes, her sister's husband had just died, to which he replied stolidly that a sister's husband wasn't a very close member of the family. Callous creature.

I had a blood test done at the Polyclinic last week. As usual, my veins refused to flow and I needed many new jabs. I was amused to see that though the young woman had an impressive array of tubes and pipettes, she apparently had no scissors, and was obliged to tear and bite the strips of bandage with which she bound me at the conclusion!

Howard arrives tomorrow at lunchtime and I have not yet wrapped my Christmas presents, so I had better stop and get on with the job.

Much love from us both,

Nao

Moscow

29 December 1958

My dear Ma, Pa, and Liz,

Oh dear, oh dear, only fifteen minutes till the bag leaves, and this is the first time I have had a chance to sit down at my desk since Christmas. As you know as a result of having tried to phone us, we have been at home very little all week. What a pity, when there is so much news to relate and such wonderful presents to thank you for. I want to comment on each one of them — you *did* choose cleverly — and I think the best thing is to send this now and to write more fully in the course of the week.

Meanwhile, a general "thank you" for all the gifts, and also for the phone call, which I particularly appreciate. So sorry that you had to try so many times, and even spent one call talking to someone else.

I am exhausted from parties and from droppers-in who stay till all hours (though I am otherwise in good health). But we are enjoying Howard, who is a wonderfully easy guest and who brought a ton of provisions from Helsinki with him.

More, much more, next week. Thank you again for all your kindnesses, and much love,

Nao.

Moscow

2 January 1959

My dear Parents and Liz,

Your presents were all of them small strokes of genius — eminently useful and at the same time complete surprises. I had of course coveted Pa's baggage-weigher since I first saw it; he was clever to remember. For long we have intended to buy a box for our photographic slides; now clever Ma has filled that gap, and very handsomely. And Lizzie's corkscrew works, really works, leaving no cork residue in the drink. Moreover, Howard and Max tell me that no other type is used in the best restaurants in Paris nowadays. Finally, our living room is now resplendent with an array of gramophone records in Lizzie's rack, which is just what we need-ed. So thanks to all of you, not only for those gifts but for all the kind things you have done during the year and undertaken to do during the coming year.

Not the least of these was your telephone call last week. It wasn't a very coherent conversation but I gathered you had phoned partly to offer con-gratulations, and thank you for that. Isn't it a bit terrifying to be almost a grandfather and a grandmother, not to mention an aunt? Next time you come to Russia they will call you "babushka" and "dedushka" and "tyotushka." We are beginning to wonder if it isn't all a false alarm (although the Doc insists not), because Na seems in excellent health all day long. I thought she was supposed to be ghastly ill every morning and go about all day craving pickles. Maybe that comes later.

We have had rather a nasty financial blow connected with the baby business. Ontario has put a free hospital system into effect. Alarmed by this, the health insurance scheme to which we have long subscribed has pulled out of Ontario altogether, leaving us high and dry so far as surgery and obstetrics are concerned. I promptly signed up for a new scheme, but like all the others this one gives no obstetrical benefits for the first nine months after you have joined. This raises the question of National Health benefits in England. Is Nao eligible for the services of a doctor courtesy of the National Health? If so, our insurance problems won't matter so much. When it comes to the hospital room, as opposed to the obstetrical charges, we are well covered.

(Continued a day later.)

Howard's visit ends tonight; he's been here nearly two weeks and we liked having him. There was an unfortunate muddle at the end, which pre-vented his seeing Leningrad: the Foreign Ministry decided that he was a diplomat rather than a tourist and must therefore give advance notice and all that. But it turned out all right in the end, because we got tickets for *Swan Lake* tonight. He would otherwise have seen no ballet, only an opera.

We've enjoyed having the Stratford performers here. Our Posol had twenty of them to Christmas dinner, together with all the Canadian staff, and we have seen quite a lot of them on other occasions. At the Bolshoi the other night we picked up Romeo and the Nurse and Maria (*Twelfth Night*) and a nice young man with a lot of hair and only walk-on parts, and brought them back here for drinks. They seemed to be glad. Romeo is a saturnine youth and is reliably reported to be in love with Juliet (Dorothy Tutin). I have never been at close quarters with actors before and was surprised at how normal they were. A few artsy-crafty types, but not bad and not many. We managed to get tickets to all three plays (*R.& J.* and *T.N.* and *Hamlet*), though I personally am free to see only the last.

Max and I are off on the first trip of the year shortly, returning just before the Party Congress on January 27th. We will be away only four days, but all travel will be by air, so that we shall have enough time in Kiev and Lvov, where we are going once again to pay pensions. Kiev I have already seen, but no more of Lvov than the airport, and people say that it is interesting and comfortable.

We both send our love and good wishes for the year to all of you.

Peter.

P.S. from me, Naomi

I endorse all Peter's comments on your well-chosen presents, and I add my thanks for the beautiful lengths of dress material for Janice and for me, and for my new pocket diary. I have enjoyed arranging our records in Liz's record rack, and I have made a fine display of the artificial lilies of the valley in the handsome Finnish glass vase that Howard gave me, even adding water to increase the illusion that they are fresh flowers. The only item that is not at present in use is the golfball-like plug, which, alas, does not fit our hand basin, but will travel with us to be tested in other basins and bathtubs. Meanwhile, we are quite used to making do with our tin basin, though Howard at first took a dim view of our washing facilities.

I am afraid our gifts to you were very humble.

Moscow
5 January 1959

My dear Families,

I have got so behind in telling the news that I am going to do a joint letter, so if I repeat what some of you have already heard from me or from Pete, just skip that part. (I hope my version corresponds with Peter's — you never know.)

I will go back to the 23rd of December, when Howard arrived at noon, bearing with him $80.00 worth of wonderful fresh meat and frozen fish, plus a great load of fresh and frozen fruit and vegetables, of which he made me a present (the fruit and veg.). We delivered the food to the Embassy, then the three of us went off with Don Knox in his car to have lunch at his apartment. He is the Canadian Naval Attaché and accredited to Helsinki as well as to Moscow, so he and his wife Ann know Howard well.

After lunch Howard, Nina, and I stored the food to be frozen in the deep freeze, then the Yaldens came to supper and shared our fresh salad and fresh fruit. Afterwards, Peter, Max, and Howard went off on some ghastly binge in Moscow's nightspots, during which they had a series of adventures, and Janice and I wrapped up Christmas presents. Then Janice went home, but not to sleep, as the men returned there very rowdy at about 2:00 a.m. and demanded to be fed. I've forgotten at what time P. and H. arrived back here, but I think pretty late.

The next day Peter worked in the office and the Crowes came to lunch. After supper Peter and Howard went to the famous puppet show. At midnight we all three went to the British Embassy for the midnight service, and afterwards walked some of the way home while searching for a taxi, and very cold it was, but fun. We had a nightcap, then went to bed until about 11:00 a.m. the next day.

After breakfast we had the ceremonial present-opening at home, then there was just time to change for lunch at the Ambassador's at 1:30. In addition to all the Canadian staff and a couple of Canadian visitors who had got stranded in Moscow, Posol had invited twenty or more of the actors and stage hands from the Stratford company, who had arrived in Moscow that week. You should have heard the complaints that the Ambassador was "spoiling our Christmas by making us play host to a lot of strangers" — whereas in fact the strangers were quite delightful and made the Christmas party twice as much fun as last year's had been! Now the former complainers are being very smug and saying how wicked it was of the British Ambassador to have neglected the troupe on Christmas Day (though in fact the British between them entertained all seventy-five of the troupe on Boxing Day).

Well, anyway, the Canadians and the Stratford people were split up at a number of small tables and we had a good Christmas meal, partly served and partly buffet style. Among those at my table were Michael Redgrave (Hamlet) and Michael Meecham (Paris and Orsino and Guildenstern) and Ron Heddrick (Horatio and Tybalt and one other), and they were very co-operative and animated as regards conversation, even exchanging riddles at the end of the meal. (I scored top marks with Pa's "What is it that flies and swims and has three corners?") Then after the meal we retired to The Tree and the Ambassador gave out presents to the wives and to the Russian staff, and a pot of caviar to each of the Stratford guests.

At about five o'clock the party broke up, and at nine we went for Christmas supper to the Yaldens, from which the three of us finally got home at 5:00 a.m.

The next day we got up rather late, and after lunch went to George's to deliver our Christmas presents. By great good luck, his mysterious artist protégé, whom we have wanted to meet for so long, was paying a visit, and George asked him to paint our portraits, which he did, taking about five minutes to do each one. He spread large sheets of paper on the floor and painted one of his queer sloshy efforts of each of us, and we can tell which is which, but no one else could, or could even guess that it was a portrait at all, but in addition he did a more conventional sketch of me, which is really very clever, and funny too. Anyway, it was exciting to meet Zverev at last. (Note to Mother and Mary: we have bought or been given by George several of this artist's pictures, some of which we like very much. George swears that they will be worth a fortune one day — and he is usually right on such matters.)

In the evening of Boxing Day we went to a dinner at the McAlpines (British), where the guests included more Stratford people, and from there on to the Commonwealth dance at the British Ambassador's residence, but we stayed only an hour there, as we wanted to drop in on the Crowes to pay our respects. We were in bed comparatively early that night — about 1:00 or 2:00 a.m., I think.

The next day Doris and I went at 9:00 a.m. to the wedding in the Catholic church of our Iranian friend and her Austrian. It was a depressing affair, for not one of Irene's family or the Embassy staff turned up. They disapprove strongly of the marriage, as she ought to be a good Moslem and not a Catholic of recent conversion. That evening Peter and I and the Crowes went to the wedding reception that Irene's parents gave for her, but it again was rather depressing, as it was deliberately made to appear just like any old cocktail party, with no wedding speeches or toasts, and one obviously could not say the usual polite things to the parents of the bride. After the reception there was a small party at the Yaldens for us, the Costakis family, the Crowes, and John Fast.

On Sunday we three and the Yaldens went to a lovely concert of chamber music and then to a Russian restaurant, which wasn't as bad as usual, in fact Howard thinks we make a lot of fuss about nothing.

On Monday I took Howard shopping in the morning and we gave a farewell lunch of ten people for John Fast. Nina prepared one of the beautiful roasts of beef that Howard had brought, and she overcooked it by one full hour. To be fair, it is unlike Nina to do such a thing, and I am sure it won't happen again.

At night we three walked to the local theatre in the coldest weather we have had for weeks (but the theatre is only ten minutes' walk away) and saw Dostoyevsky's *Idiot* — or, rather, we saw the first act, which lasted two hours, and decided to skip the other two acts. It was quite good, but hard to follow, especially for Howard, of course. We were home by 10:00 p.m. and in bed by midnight, a record.

On Tuesday morning I took Howard shopping again and we all attended the Ambassador's lunch for the new Soviet Ambassador to Canada. He and his wife are both Armenians, and seem rather nice, especially the wife. All three of the Foreign Ministry officials who deal with Canada came too, and all brought their wives, which is very unusual. It went pretty well on the whole.

After lunch I took Howard out again, then P. and I very fleetingly attended a farewell cocktail party for the Puttevils, a well-liked Belgian couple who are off to Brussels, where he is to be the assistant to the President. From there we whizzed over to the Yaldens' to munch a sandwich, pick up Howard, and leave, all five of us, for the Bolshoi to hear *Prince Igor*. It was not enjoyable, and we left at the end of the second act, bearing off with us four Stratford people, who were equally bored with the Opera. They were: Angela Baddeley (Juliet's nurse and the wife of the Director), Richard Johnson (Romeo), Geraldine McEwan (Olivia), and John Grayson (a Capulet servant). We served them drinks and toasted cheese sandwiches, and they stayed a couple of hours. I think they were quite pleased to be elsewhere than in their hotel. They are remarkably agreeable, though I find Romeo a bit sultry; he is reputed to be really in love with Juliet, Dorothy Tutin, and vice versa, which all adds to the fun.

Wednesday was New Year's Day and I sent Howard off on his own to see the Kremlin and its museum, which he did very diligently and observantly. At night we went to an excellent New Year party at the Thomases', dinner first, then dancing for those who wanted to. After their performance, some of the Stratford people joined the party, among whom a few we felt by this time we could call our friends. It was very pleasant altogether, but we left at about 1:30, for we had promised the Yaldens that we would drop in on the Crowes, where they expected to be after they had all been to the theatre together. We found the Yaldens still there and were able to wish a happy new year all round.

The next day even Howard was beginning to show signs of wear and tear. We did nothing in the morning, but in the afternoon we drove out to the airport to see off the Puttevils and to buy Howard some caviar to take home. Then we went on to a small and pleasant little party at the Lamberts' (he is the *N.Y. Herald Tribune* man), but we could only stay a few minutes, as we were expected to dinner at the Knoxes'. Howard very sensibly fell asleep soon after arrival, and was consequently fresh again when Ann served her excellent dinner. Afterwards Don showed us some quite interesting films and slides that he had made of his trips in the S.U. (the attachés travel much more than the other diplomats do), and we left for home at about midnight.

Friday was supposed to be Howard's last day — he was to leave in the evening and spend the next day in Leningrad. However, the Foreign Ministry claimed that he was a diplomat, not a tourist, and would not allow *Burobin* to sell him a ticket without the usual forty-eight hours' notice that we residents have to give. I had invited the Yaldens to a farewell dinner for Howard, so they came anyway, even if it wasn't to say farewell. We had a real *filet* of beef (cooked by me this time), and it was wonderful, especially when accompanied by fresh frozen broccoli.

On Saturday Peter stayed in bed late, as he was not on duty, but the usual demands by the office staff for his signature and on other matters started at 10:30, and I had to disturb him so many times that he might as well have got up. Howard was feeling pretty exhausted too. It wasn't until five o'clock that the ticket business was satisfactorily sorted out, and after that P. and Howard went for a walk while I prepared supper and rested. P. and I and the Yaldens had tickets for the Stratford *Romeo* that night, but Peter gave his ticket to Lilya and got other tickets for himself and Howard to see *Swan Lake*. Apparently it was a simply marvellous performance, and Howard would far rather have seen it than have spent the day in Leningrad.

Peter saw Howard onto his train and then drove to the Yaldens' for a late-night supper. They and I had just arrived after our show. The enthusiasm to see the English company is fantastic. I was aware that it was very difficult to get tickets, but I had not been prepared for the mob outside the theatre struggling to buy tickets at black market prices from those who were lucky enough to have been able to obtain some. I was a little disappointed in *Romeo and Juliet*, but they say *Hamlet* is better (we are going tonight), and *Twelfth Night* best of all. As a treat for Lilya we went round backstage afterwards and introduced her to some of the actors, and she was very thrilled.

Yesterday, Sunday, we did nothing at all, except to go for a walk in the evening gloaming and to try to find Tolstoy's house, only it was closed by the time we got there. We had a wonderfully peaceful day, ending with a supper of fresh frozen sole, courtesy of Howard.

Now that I come to write of all these activities I no longer wonder that we seem to have been rather busy during the last two weeks. But it was fun, and Howard was a most easy and cheerful guest. I haven't seen Peter so merry in ages as he was while he and Howard were fooling at the piano. Luckily, I am feeling well, otherwise I could never have kept up the pace. Now we plan to have a quiet week — I hope.

Much love to you all,

Ever,

Naomi.

<hr />

Moscow

11 January 1959

My dear Parents and Liz,

I'm afraid I haven't very good news to offer this time. Naomi lost the baby on Friday. She is in hospital now and is all right herself (but weak); there is some suggestion that she will be allowed to come home tomorrow.

At the beginning the British doctor thought there was some chance of keeping the baby, and ordered Naomi into bed and absolute quiet. But by Friday morning she was losing a great deal of blood, so we had the ambulance come and Naomi aborted in the Russian hospital, where she still is. I think, and so does she, that the Russian doctors are very competent and there is no doubt she is getting good treatment. You needn't be uneasy on that score. But of course it is very disappointing and discouraging.

There is however a somewhat brighter side. Both the British and Soviet doctors say that it will not be difficult, in a few months' time, to correct the internal condition that brought on the trouble, a retroverted uterus. The British doctor told me that most often this condition corrects itself during pregnancy. Nao's did not. She has had a fairly bad time of it, of course, a lot of really severe pain, which is not over yet.

I realize how sad this is for you. But it is only a temporary setback, and with any kind of luck things should work out well next time.

Please don't mind this very short letter. It's dashed off between visits to the hospital, in order to catch tomorrow's bag.

Warmest love from both of us,

Peter

<hr />

Moscow
17 January 1959

Dear Families,

Here is a joint letter to tell you what happened to me last week. Some of it Peter has probably told you already, so excuse me if this is repetitive. Also, I'm very sorry that I frustrated your grandmotherly, grandfatherly, and auntly ambitions, but I think it was inevitable, and that my activity at Christmastime did not really make any difference to the outcome. My health was in fact very good during pregnancy, much better than usual, and my hair even began to curl again!

Peter has certainly told you that the trouble was caused by a retroverted uterus. The doc was hoping the uterus would flip over in the fourth month, and if not he would have tried to manipulate it, but he did not want to touch it before the end of the third month, by which time the baby would have become nicely established. However, near the end of the third month the baby woke up to the fact that it was getting trapped in the pelvic region (pretty smart, at minus six months of age), and started agitating to be let out; "fear of incarceration" is the correct term, I'm told. This began in the early morning of Thursday January 8th; the doc came twice and gave me various shots, and by nighttime he could express the situation in these words: "You are just holding your own, but it is touch and go."

I had a very painful night, and by eight the next morning I was obviously in labour (though I didn't at the time realize that this was the cause of those particular pains). At about 10:30 an ambulance arrived and two men carried me out on a stretcher. As so often occurs in the S.U., they gave every appearance of being on the job for the first time, and it was no surprise when one of them dropped his end of the stretcher. We arrived at the Reception Department of the hospital (George Costakis kindly drove over and joined me at this point), and at about 11:00 a.m. I gave birth to the baby, which I and several worthy Moscow citizens who were milling about the room in their street clothes then inspected. (Hygiene and privacy are comparatively undeveloped features of Soviet medicine.) Incidentally, I heard later that the baby was "normal," sex undeterminable at that stage.

I was wheeled off almost immediately to the operating theatre to be cleaned out, an operation that is performed here under local anaesthetic, just a jab of novocaine on the surface area. It lasted only about fifteen minutes, but pretty nasty all the same. I noticed that the instruments were brought in uncovered from somewhere outside the room, so I was glad of the three precautionary penicillin jabs a day that were administered while I was in the hospital.

The worst part followed the cleaning-out operation (a D. and C., I suppose we would call it, though mercifully the D. had already taken place). The lady doctor left the operating room, trusting me to the care of the two junior staff. They were to wheel me out of the theatre, but they began to squabble about whether or not I should be allowed to keep the blanket that covered me. Would they get into trouble if they lost track of operating theatre property? One was concerned for the patient's comfort, the other was anxious about having to account for the blanket. In the end I summoned all my language skills and said, "I am keeping the blanket." They were immensely relieved that the patient had taken responsibility, and wheeled me out with friendly goodbyes.

So far so good, but the proper authorities had not been alerted, and there I remained in the corridor for more than two hours (I was still wearing my watch), by now in ever-increasing pain. I occasionally tried to stop a passerby in order to beg for a painkilling pill, but they just shrugged because it was none of their business. (I attribute the fact that I was left like this not to neglect or indifference, but just to administrative muddle; a person in the corridor belongs to neither one department nor another.) Finally my moans became so loud that a dear old thing who was standing guard in the corridor took pity on me and telephoned someone or other and told him or her to hurry up and take me to the sanatorium. (She was, I think, a quite lowly employee, but sufficiently aged to remember the olden days, when perhaps individuals dared to take the initiative.) Almost at once two men came and wheeled me away, back to the original public room where I had first been examined, and after five minutes or so there I was put into an ambulance and driven over to the foreigners' Korpus of the hospital.

Now things got much better. I was put to bed in a room by myself, was given a wonderfully effective painkiller (what a relief, at last) and at three o'clock Peter arrived, looking just as white as I was.

The hospital was not at all bad, really. Most of the nurses were very sweet, though I doubt that they had been given much training, for they became very upset when facing any emergency. The doctors, too, were nice (all women), but I found they had the habit of examining too much and too often. If they found a sore spot that made me jump and shriek they would probe and probe at that spot, as if it helped to clarify their diagnosis. I rarely saw the same doctor twice, and as there appeared to be no shared patient records I had to tell my story afresh at each visit. This was a bit of a challenge, for our language of communication might be Russian, German, or French, but almost never English.

There were reminders on a practical level that this was not a Western hospital; for instance, there were no bed-trays, never mind bed-tables (food was just left on a table near to the bed), the sheets and towels were not changed during the six days I was resident, the bed was of the army-cot type, sunk in the middle, and so on and so on. On the other hand, all the staff were most anxious to please, and I am sure they would have provided me with clean bed linen had I asked. In some ways they treat the patient as being more intelligent than Western doctors and nurses usually do, for they always tell you what your temperature is without your asking, and they tell you what the pills and injections are that they are giving you. Also, they don't bring breakfast until 9:00 a.m., and they don't bother you until that time unless to administer medicines, and they let you turn off your own light when you are ready at night. (I suppose this may not be the case in a public ward.)

Anyway, to cut a long story short, I remained in the hospital until Wednesday, sometimes in pain and sometimes not, while they pumped all kinds of serums into me. Then on the Wednesday I suddenly felt much better and asked to be let out. They found that I could still be made to jump and shriek upon examination and they were longing to give me an electric cauterization (I think). But I said no, please, I want to go home, and they obligingly said O.K., but come and see us in a couple of weeks. So I phoned Peter to ask him to bring me some clothes, and in a couple of hours we were at home, and I never saw a place look so beautiful.

Well, the outcome of all this is that I shall probably go to Helsinki in March or April in order to have my uterus sewn to face the way it ought to, a quite common operation, I believe, and after that all will be plain sailing. The operation is also performed in the S.U., under local anaesthetic, but I think once is enough for me. So it's to Helsinki I shall go, where I understand that they have a lovely hospital and a good doctor.

Thus, although you are not immediately to become grandparents and aunts, I feel that we are further ahead than we were three months ago (for it was the longest short-term pregnancy I have yet achieved), and it has therefore not been an entirely wasted experience, albeit an unpleasant one. Let's view it as a practice run.

I'm sorry if I have reported all this in too much detail. I rather wanted to have a record of the events for my own interest.

I will be answering your many letters individually later on, so that's all for the joint letter.

Much love,

Nao.

◆◆

Moscow

19 January 1959

My dear Parents and Liz,

I have a great pile of letters from you to be answered, so this will be pretty disjointed.

First, thank you for telephoning on Wednesday. I ought to have phoned you myself and indeed I did think of it, but felt too tired, and thought that a tired voice would give you the impression that I was not better. In fact I was better, and am now much better yet. I am still taking life very easy, but am really in perfectly good health again.

I am not feeling as depressed as you might think; it is so great to be out of pain and out of the hospital that my spirits are unreasonably high. Speaking of pain, I still marvel at the effectiveness of the tiny pill that was given to me when I was first taken to my hospital room. For, as we may have told you, over-the-counter painkillers are unavailable to regular citizens, and many times members of our local staff have begged us for an aspirin or a 222 when they are suffering. We dare not hand out more than one or two pills at a time, for fear they might in all innocence give leftover pills to a child and do serious damage. If I provide a pill it is always accompanied by a stern caution.

I am afraid that Mother Roberts is not anxious to make the proposed trip to Britain in June, after all. Even with our help, it would cripple her financially for years to come, and since her pension is pretty small, she does not want to take any risks. I think she does not really want to cash our cheque, either. She is very apologetic, and leaves it up to us to make the final decision, but we do not want to persuade her against her better judgment. There may be other opportunities, and she certainly is not dull or idle at home. Too bad, but perhaps the idea alone has helped to tide her over a difficult time. I think we will still take some leave in June, but perhaps not the whole month now.

I'm sorry, Ma, if you feel that you purchased new mattresses in vain, in honour of the special visitor, but I assure you, you *did* need them. The only mattress I know as uncomfortable as the Eton Road ones was the one I slept on in the hospital!

Thanks so much to all of you for choosing and sending such appropriate presents to the Crowe family. The children gobbled up their books and have played the record of Christmas carols many times over. I expect Doris will write to you herself (or has done so) about your gifts to her and Marshall. They entertained at Christmas dinner the Wembley Lions hockey team, all of them Canadian players. The Crowes are delighted to be going home (not just on home leave), even though they will have made two moves in the course of one year, no easy task for a family of six.

I don't think I told you how splendid Nina was while I was away. She worked like a Trojan, washed all my sweaters and cardigans, and polished all the floors as a "surprise" for Madame. She wept copiously when they carried me off, and again when Peter told her that I had lost the baby. Her stony heart is only for surface wear; inside she is just as emotional as most Russians.

I enjoyed the Sally Belfrage book; her stories ring true and she writes wittily. Her comments on the American Embassy, however, are so very unfair that one wonders slightly how accurate some of her assessments of the Russians can be. Of course there are people still around here who met her during the Festival, or later. The journalist with whom she stayed at first was Ralph Parker, and he was instrumental in getting her the job in the Publishing House.

That's all I have time for now. I must go and rest, having been out of bed for all of five hours!

Much love,

Nao.

Moscow

25 January 1959

My dear Families,

I wrote such long letters last week that there is almost nothing to say today.

The temperature has suddenly shot up several degrees, so that it feels like spring, which it can't possibly be yet, but even this phony spring is a wonderful break.

Whether because of the weather, or because of the enforced rest of the past weeks, or for some other reason, I am feeling and looking remarkably well, and am enjoying seeing company again after having been out of circulation for a while. I still get up rather late, but feel less and less need to rest. This is a relief, because for the first ten days or so after losing the baby I felt so weak that I couldn't help wondering how I would manage if I had a baby to look after as well as my own needs and Peter's to consider, but my friends who are mothers assure me that they felt equally tired and useless for the first while, but that one does recover from it, and I see that they are right.

Peter and Max left on Thursday night for Kiev, where some of their Canadian pensioners were to come and meet them, and yesterday they flew to Lvov for the same purpose. They telephoned last night, but I was out. However, Janice took the call (she is staying here while Max is away), and she spoke to them both. They seem to be having a lovely time and to like Lvov. They are due home on Monday night. It is good for both of them to get away from Moscow for a few days. My non-pregnant state means that I too am able to do some travelling in the S.U. this year, and I hope it comes to pass.

What a pity that I started on this big sheet of paper, because I can't think of a single piece of news. Better luck next week.

Much love,

Nao

P.S. to Zimans: David F. telephoned this morning. I have decided that the best thing to do is to behave as if I had heard nothing about his professional spat with Pa, and he will doubtless be with us next week.

———

Moscow

31 January 1959

My dear Parents and Liz,

This is Crowe departure day; they leave by train for Helsinki tonight, just one year after they arrived. They are thoroughly disillusioned, for they came full of enthusiasm, in spite of their previous posting here in 1948-51. They were convinced that there had been some real changes in the country, which of course there have not. Marshall is, rightly, regarded as a brain in the Department, and a coming man; he has found the work frustrating after New York, and Doris is fed up for half a dozen reasons, not the least being the fact that she has never been out of Moscow nor escaped the demands of her numerous family since they arrived. (As you know, the parents did not make the anticipated trip to London last November.) There will be a great gathering at the station tonight, because they are well known and well liked in Moscow, and many people sought Marshall's opinions on all sorts of matters.

The current ailment in these parts is flu, and Nao is in bed with it, like nearly all the rest of the diplomatic corps and half the population of Moscow. They have even begun closing schools, a rare thing here. It seems to be a fairly mild virus, so Nao isn't feeling too sorry for herself, and is able to read quite happily in bed. I had it three weeks ago and hope to escape this time.

David F. rang up one day last week and came around to chat about the Congress. He's here on a visitor's visa again, and therefore isn't admitted to the Congress nor allowed to file, but he seems well informed anyway and gave us a few useful tips. I think he's an able chap; it's too bad he blotted his copybook by getting into a snit because of Pa's temporary intrusion into his bailiwick. (There's one for the metaphor book.) We invited him to dinner, but he backed out at the last minute, claiming that he would try to see us when he got back from Leningrad next week.

We eat and sleep only Congress these days. Each morning *Pravda* publishes ten or twelve pages of the previous day's speeches, and our task (Max's and mine) is to wade through this and by noon to have an *en clair* outline of what matters on its way to Ottawa, where it will be waiting for people when they come to work at 9:00 a.m. Naturally Khrushchev himself said pretty well all there was to say, but the foreign Communists, especially Chou, added a certain amount. Our ordinary work is getting far behind and when the Congress finishes there will be a great rush to catch up.

Naomi probably told you that Max and I went last week on a four-day trip to Kiev and Lvov. It was good fun. We called on and had a friendly chat with the Chief of Protocol of the Ukrainian Foreign Ministry; we spent an evening at the University talking to the English Department and watching a student play; we ate in a very good restaurant where the band played "St. Louis Blues," "Ole Torero," and "My Red Wagon"; and we managed to fly from Kiev to Lvov on a plane that was forced by bad weather to land in Stanislav, a closed city in a closed area unvisited by foreigners since the war. In Lvov we admired the buildings, which are superb (seventeenth- and eighteenth-century Austrian in the centre, twentieth-century Polish in the suburbs, no Soviet buildings at all), and made friends with an Aeroflot pilot, who got drunk on a combination of vodka and Scotch and had to be taken home (by me) and put to bed. His digs-mate was another pilot, a Jew, who told me that there is strong anti-Semitism in the Soviet Union, not on the part of the government, but among the people.

Apart from the food, everything about the trip was splendid, although it should of course have been a lot longer, so that we could also have visited Uzhgorod, Cherovitsy, and Kishinev, which cities they say are as amusing as Lvov.

Our plans for the February holiday (our "breath of fresh air") are still fluid as to dates and places, but there is no question that we shall be leaving. On the way to London we expect to spend a day or two in Copenhagen, mainly in order to visit our Ambassador there, John Watkins, one of the ablest and most amiable people in the Department. He used to be Chargé d'Affaires and then Ambassador here in Moscow, and had a phenomenal success.

Love to you all,
Peter

———   ———

Moscow
9 February 1959

My dear Parents and Liz.

Yesterday I began to feel cheerful again for the first time since my Asian flu struck, and to take an interest in my food; today I feel almost back to normal. I got up for the first full day last Wednesday, so only in fact had six days in bed, but all the victims agree that the after-effects are almost as bad as the illness itself. Almost every diplomatic family has had a member or members smitten, and among the Russians the epidemic has been so widespread that doctors who retired two years ago have been called back into service.

The good news of the week is that Mother Roberts is after all coming to Britain and has even reserved her ticket. Unexpectedly, she learned that the Department of Veterans' Affairs will continue to pay Father Roberts' full ex-service pension and this means that she is not nearly so strapped for money as she had supposed, and can afford to take one trip in her life. So, Ma, please do not cancel your request for tickets for *My Fair Lady* and for the Trooping of the Colour — on 6th June, wasn't it?

We spent a happy afternoon and evening yesterday working out an itinerary. All is subject to change, however, as it may sound to Mrs R. like too exhausting a program, in which case we would shorten our proposed tour of Britain and spend longer in London.

We were discussing this trip as we walked home after having visited Tolstoy's house, and Peter commented that the Three Feathers in Ludlow, a sixteenth-century inn, was far advanced in its original architecture and furnishings and amenities as compared with the nineteenth-century Tolstoy house. As a museum it was quite interesting, the most striking feature (to me) being the maid's sleeping quarters — on top of a *trunk* behind a screen in the pantry! And Tolstoy was known for his advanced notions regarding the condition of the peasants.

David F. dropped in twice last week to see Peter. I was still sick in bed, and he was afraid of my germs, so we just shouted at one another through the bedroom door. P. thinks that David would be quite glad to bury hatchets now. Has he spoken to Pa?

No news that I can think of. I shall probably arrive in London on February 26th or 27th. I wish Peter could come too, as he is in sore need of a break, but I daresay even the one week that he will take in Germany will do the trick. He is going there in order to purchase the VW we have chosen and to organize temporary storage for it.

Much love,
Naomi

——◆——

Moscow
16 February 1959

My dear Ma and Pa,

Thank you for Ma's letters of 29 January and 4 February and for Pa's of 5 February.

Okay, okay, I agree to see a specialist in London, if Cousin Henry will recommend one, and to ask whether said specialist is free to do the surgery in March. You are right, it probably would be more practical all round if I can have the operation done in London, rather than in Helsinki, and as I will be a private patient it should not be too difficult to book a hospital bed. I don't think you needed to be worried about the doctor in Helsinki whom I had intended to consult, however, for he is the big chief gynecologist of all Finland. Nevertheless, if the business can be done in London I will be entirely satisfied, and it will be especially nice if you can come and visit me in hospital.

Are you going to provide fine weather for me? I am truly looking forward to my visit. I haven't any special plans; it will be enough of a treat just to be there with you. I will let you know by telegram or letter just which day to expect me.

Poor Ma, working yourself to a standstill in an effort to make the house "Canadian-clean" in honour of Mother Roberts. I am quite recovered in health so will be able to help you a bit when I come (although I am sadly out of practice when it comes to shuffling the dust around).

We had intended to make a weekend trip to Riga, leaving last Friday, to which I was much looking forward. However, Posol asked Peter to prepare a dispatch on the economic aspects of the Party Congress in time for today's bag, and if he had not worked on it during Saturday and Sunday he would not have got it done, so we had to give up the trip.

Tomorrow we are giving a lunch for Harry, one of the Chancery guards, who is leaving Moscow on Wednesday. We have invited most of the Canadian office staff and some of his British friends.

No, Macmillan's visit is not likely to affect the Canadians (luckily for us and our holiday). Sir Fitzroy Maclean is coming later.

See you soon.

Love from us both,

Naomi

Moscow
13 April 1959

My dear Ma, Pa and Liz,

Not much time to write, as my bag day will be taken up with the writing of business letters, but I want to send you a note just to say many, many thanks for looking after me so nicely and for sending me back feeling (and looking) better than I have for at least a year. Dima II (not the Ambassador's Dima) couldn't get over my appearance: he walked around me several times exclaiming admiringly.

The surgery, as you know, was more elaborate than we had been led to expect. "Like unpicking a fine piece of crochet work," is how the surgeon described his delicate task of releasing the multitude of adhesions. (I don't think you ever met the elegant silver-haired Mr Jackson. My roommates used to swoon when he entered the ward in his well-cut suit, a fresh flower in his buttonhole.)

I was especially glad to have your company during the days of discomfort. Once the pain had lessened I enjoyed also the company of my fellow-patients in the ward; they were a jolly lot. Best of all was the experience of convalescing at home. Liz, special thanks to you for having taken me on that little holiday to Rye, a place I had never visited before but now intend to recommend to visitors to Britain. My memories of the hospital experience and the recovery period are by no means all bad.

The journey back from Brussels was wonderful. It was perfect flying weather, and I was able to watch the Soviet Union unroll at my feet. I especially enjoyed seeing Riga from the air. I almost had all eighty places to myself, but the only other booked passenger turned up, panting heavily, ten minutes after takeoff time, and the plane had waited for her. I did not speak to her on the plane, but when we reached Moscow I tried to take her under my wing, for she seemed totally bewildered. She was an elderly woman from Boston who spoke English with a strange accent (Armenian, I learned). She was coming to visit her two sisters in Yerevan, whom she had not seen for many years. I hope to goodness she has an exit visa. She was expecting to fly to Yerevan that same evening, but I think she and Thomas Cook in London were a bit optimistic about the amount of assistance she was going to receive at Moscow airport.

Nina was touchingly pleased to see me back, and I don't know how we are going to break it to her that she must leave our service. But go she must, for according to the new order of things she now costs us a third of our total allowances. Also, there is really not enough for her to do, and there will be still less when we lose our sitting room, as we expect to do very soon. We hope to arrange for some help with cleaning for a few hours each week, and I can very well cope with the rest. But oh, how hard to fire our Nina, even though we may have had our differences over time.

How did you enjoy your respective weekends, Pa in Brussels, Ma in Kent, and Liz in London? I hope you are all able to have a more restful time now that your invalid has departed. Thanks, Pa, for accompanying me to Brussels, and thanks again to all of you for your goodness and loving kindness.

Lots of love from Pete and me,

Naomi.

——~ ~——

Moscow

13 April 1959

My dear Ma,

This is to wish you a happy birthday come April 17, and to thank you and Pa and Liz for doing so well by Nao. She is positively blooming, looking like a kid, and I think that the fact that serious summer began on the very day she returned will help to keep her that way. Everyone is glad to see her back, naturally, and the Russians especially have gone into fits of delight at how well she looks.

The trouble with this life is that it never lets you alone. We are faced now with the job of adjusting to a radical reduction in our allowances and an even more radical one in our living accommodation. It is going to be *so* good to shake the dust of this place for a whole month in June and to leave the wretched housekeeping problems behind.

Please thank Pa from me for looking after Na as far as Brussels, and give him and Liz and the cat my love. And again, many happies to you and much gratitude to you all.

Affectionately,

Peter

Moscow
20 April 1959

My dear Ma, Pa and Liz,

I have been trapped in "your" bedroom for the past hour, separated from my writing things, while Peter has a meeting in the sitting room with our latest Inspection Team, and that is why this letter is written in pencil, not, as you thought, because I am sick in bed.

In fact my health continues good, though I naturally have little reserves of energy even yet. Peter is very strict with me and comes down from the office to pay me surprise visits in the afternoon, to see if he can catch me *not* resting, but he hasn't caught me yet. Nina comes in early each day to prepare Peter's breakfast, so I don't need to get up until I want to do so, and I go to bed at ten o'clock or even earlier. This does not leave much of a day, and consequently I achieve very little, but no matter. My Ghastly Wound is no longer ghastly, and is practically cured.

With great trepidation we gave Nina notice for the end of this month, but she took the news quite calmly — indeed, had been expecting it, I think, ever since the Yaldens dismissed their maid. But after seeing me look tired one day after I had boiled an egg or engaged in some equally exhausting activity, Peter changed his mind and told Nina we would keep her until June, and she was very pleased, and I too. Actually, we are in a good position, living in the embassy itself, because George thinks that Katya, the embassy cleaning woman, will be willing to come in for two hours each day to clean and wash dishes for me, which will leave me only the cooking to do, and I quite enjoy that.

What's more, thanks to the bright idea of one of the current Inspectors, there is a chance that we may keep our sitting room after all, which will save a heap of trouble. Jim Barker cleverly thought of making a sort of public dining room downstairs into an office, instead of converting our room for the same purpose. Naturally Posol is against the proposal — "Where will the Girls be able to eat their sandwiches?" — but since it will save the Government the cost of a new flat for our successor, perhaps the idea will be put into effect in spite of his objections. All this is pure speculation as yet.

We are seeing quite a lot of Jim and his companion, who is an ex-RCMP officer of many years' service, a very courteous, pleasant man, and a grandfather. It is nice to be in a position to entertain such amiable strangers to Moscow. Though, after being away for two months, I am thrilled to see even the old familiar faces.

The sole party I have attended was a tiny dinner party given by Alan Urwick, where the only other guests were Dave Mark and Miss Baeren-sprung and Henry Shapiro. I enjoyed talking and listening to all four, though I am so out of touch that half the time I can't understand what the local experts are talking about! In case I have never told you about Miss Baeren-sprung, she is the only female officer we know among the Western diplomats; she is very serious but easy to talk to and not at all conceited. (Question: when she is invited to a Men's Lunch, i.e., a lunchtime professional get-together, do they change the name of the event? I will have to ask her.)

Ida Chagall is expected in Moscow shortly, on a visit, according to George, and if she permits it we want to use her as an excuse for a small cocktail party. Is she likely to respond to Pa's name, or is your acquaintance with her too slight?

Then on 29th April we are giving a buffet dinner for sixteen, which will be the first dinner party for more than twelve that I have tried. This event is for rather junior people, mostly newcomers. After that we will be free to invite more senior people to smaller lunches and dinners. Since Peter is at present No. 2 in the mission we can and should invite people in the higher ranks. We want to get a load of entertaining done while we still have Nina to help us. (Of course we will always be able to hire extra help for entertaining as needed.)

Now that we have moved to the ten-roubles-to-one-dollar rate we need to consider more carefully the value of what we buy locally. The end of the subsidized roubles has not been fully compensated by an increase in dollars; in fact I believe that it will mean a loss of $3,000 a year for the Yaldens. We personally won't be so badly affected if we leave in September, as we have some unspent roubles in hand, in fact we may even be able to save some dollars, but it is a good thing for us that this blow was struck at the *end* of our posting.

What a tedious letter! Sorry.

Lots of love,

Nao.

～～

Moscow

27 April 1959

My dear Ma, Pa and Liz,

Did you (parents) enjoy your Devon holiday? You deserved a good holiday after having had me on your hands all that time.

I am still in good health, though I do get tired quite easily. Peter won't let me go to any cocktail parties whatever, for standing for any length of time is still something of a strain. I have been to only three dinner parties, and quite enough too.

As I told you, we are giving a big buffet dinner this week (sixteen people), as a start to repaying our long-overdue hospitality debts. We gave a small lunch last Thursday for the Yaldens and the Thomases and the Bhattys (Indian friends). The Yaldens were leaving on holiday, the Bhattys were leaving for a posting in Ankara the following day, and the Thomases will leave next month for Manila. I will try to give one more big party in May, while we still have Nina, and after that I think we will do less and less entertaining, especially if we have to move out of our sitting room. On Thursday we served the wonderful whole salmon that Howard brought us from Helsinki at Christmas, and it was much appreciated.

I had intended to give a small drinks party in honour of Miss Chagall, but she arrived later than expected, and there will be no opportunity. Peter and I met her yesterday at a dinner party given by the Costakis. She is attractive, but somehow I just did not feel at ease with her. Not that I talked to her at any length, but Peter was next to her at dinner.

Last week Jim Barker and Bob McNeill (the Inspectors) worked at the Embassy every day, and had lunch with us almost daily; as well, they dropped in for morning coffee on most days and for snacks before evenings at the ballet. We enjoyed their company, but it is nevertheless nice to be alone again. Posol was away, so Peter was in a happier mood than usual, and was able to get on with his job without constant interruption. But Posol is back now, and has moved downstairs into the office with P. (during some renovations upstairs), so if in June you fail to recognize the pale, tic-ridden creature who will accompany me, you will know the cause.

How does the house exterior look now? Mrs R. wrote recently that she would be most unhappy if she thought the Zimans were making any special preparations for her, so do make sure that the paint is dry by June, lest she think she was the cause of the facelift.

The weather here is cool but sunny and nice.

Much love,

Nao.

———

Moscow
4 May 1959

My dear Parents and Liz,

Why does Posol always invite people to lunch on a Monday, and at the last minute ask us to join him in entertaining them, thus cutting two hours off my letter-writing time on bag day?

We gave our sixteen-person dinner party last Wednesday, my biggest yet. It was buffet style, and I had cooked most of the food myself the day before, so the eating part was quite good, but the conversation part was not especially exciting. Most of our guests were newcomers to Moscow and very much on their best behaviour.

I borrowed some chairs and a table from Janice's flat, and thereby hangs a tale. I told George that I needed the Embassy truck in order to bring the chairs from the Yaldens' flat to ours, and that I would go along too, to see fair play. (As you know, the Yaldens are away on holiday.) "Then you will need two drivers," says George. "Why?" says I. "One to drive the truck and one to drive you in the car," says George. "But I shall ride in the truck," says I. "YOU CAN'T DO THAT," says George, paling at the thought. But I did, and doubtless wounded for ever his sensitive Socialist soul. It's a strange society.

The chairs and table look so nice in our sitting room that we are in no hurry to return them, but so far we have not scratched them or otherwise damaged them. (Please reassure Janice.)

We now have our marching orders regarding our return to Ottawa, and we are trying to book a passage on the *Baltika*, which sails from Leningrad on September 28th. We hope to take a couple of week's leave in Europe, and then it is *do svidanie* to the Zimans for goodness knows how long. I shan't like that.

Meanwhile, our summer leave is getting excitingly close. (Poor Yaldens, that means that their leave is drawing to an end.) Peter has to wait until Max is back, so he cannot leave for Düsseldorf (in order to pick up the Volkswagen) until Saturday May 30th.

Lots of love to you all,

Ever,

Nao.

◆～◆

Moscow
11 May 1959

My dear Ma, Pa and Liz,

Thanks, Liz, for your letter, but why do you always start off by saying "No letter from you today"? I hope you only mean that my letters are slow to reach you, for I have in fact not missed a bag day since my return (or for that matter during the whole posting, I think).

Ma, thank you very much for having invited Janice to stay until Max should arrive in London. I had a letter written on her first day, and she sounded very pleased with her accommodation. She is good company, don't you think? She clearly was blissfully happy to have found the outside world again.

Liz, there just won't be time to fit in an M.A. degree ceremony. The most we could do during this wild tour of ours would be to wave at the Vice-Chancellor in passing. On the 6th we shall be, I hope, in Penshurst, Kent, whither we are taking Aunt Maud for a night, in order to spend a few quiet hours in the country with her and Mrs R. This is at Maud's request (more or less). We are beginning to feel that the tour will wear us all out, and may therefore cancel the Scottish part, but we can decide that when we are all in London.

Alas, it now seems very unlikely that we will be able to take our remaining days of leave in October, for leave on the way home comes at the expense of the Post, and I am sure we will not be allowed to depart from Moscow early, nor would we really want to do so. All we can hope for is that there is difficulty obtaining an Atlantic crossing to coincide with the arrival of the *Baltika*, and therefore will be forced (most willingly) to mark time in London between boat journeys.

Yesterday we visited the Old Believers' Church, and also a park where we had not been before: "Izmailovski Park, called after Stalin." It is pleasant and wooded, much nicer than Gorki Park.

Much love to you all,

Ever,

Naomi

Kiev
Saturday 17 May 1959

My dear Ma, Pa and Liz,

At last I am having my long-promised trip. We flew here on Thursday night, spent all Friday in Kiev, and will fly early this evening to Odessa, from where we return to Moscow on Sunday night.

Kiev is most attractive. It is almost entirely a new city, having been largely destroyed by the Germans, but the new buildings are much more pleasing than most of the Moscow ones. Best of all, the city has a simply lovely park running along beside the river: no Culture but lots of Rest. We wandered for about three hours along treed paths (mostly chestnut trees, for which Kiev is famous), then stopped for lunch in an unusually good outdoor restaurant. More walking, then back to our hotel for glasses of tea in our room, and a rest and a bath. At about nine o'clock we went to the Dynamo Restaurant, a very modern establishment, and had an excellent meal, though much too rich for me. I had to try Chicken Kiev in Kiev, and it was good, but oh! all that squelching butter....

Sharing our table were two men, one obviously a Georgian, the other (less recognizably) a Ukrainian. The Georgian was simply immense, and it turned out that he had come to Kiev to take part in a wrestling match. We later learned that he was world champion in discus-throwing and some other kind of throwing — or else his prowess in several fields of sport made him a world champion athlete, we weren't quite sure which. He had won these honours in the 1952 Olympic games at Helsinki. Sport was his hobby, not his profession; he was in fact an engineer. In spite of being a "sportsmyen," as they say, he had a great capacity for liquor, and he treated us to one fiery drink after another. Peter was obliged to drink each toast "to the bottom." Luckily etiquette does not require women to do the same. Half a tumbler of a sort of Crème de Menthe at one gulp was almost Peter's undoing. The only consolation lay in the fact that the Ukrainian friend was in a much worse state; his eyes kept crossing — fascinating — and he was plainly feeling far from well.

We left our new chums rather precipitately, with only brief protestations of undying friendship, and set out on the long walk back to the hotel. After climbing a steep hill we met a young militiaman and asked him whether if we went straight on we would reach the centre? He replied in what I thought was an ironic tone, oh yes, we would reach the centre of the Ukraine if we kept straight on. We were about to follow his advice when he suddenly asked us in disbelief, "You weren't asking seriously, were you?" When we assured him that we were, he was even more amused, as we were walking in precisely the wrong direction if we wanted to return to the city centre.

It is now 3:30 and I have a few minutes to spare before we leave the hotel. The day has been warm, though not so sunny as yesterday, in fact a storm has just broken. Earlier, we walked in the town, which is even prettier than I had thought yesterday, chestnut trees in blossom along all the main avenues. We inspected St. Sofia's, the oldest cathedral in Russia, now a museum. We had lunch again in our open-air restaurant in the park.

Sunday

Here we are in Odessa, but I can't tell you much about it yet, as we arrived in town about nine o'clock yesterday evening and spent a long time over dinner. We have not yet been out this morning. Peter is at present trying to book our return tickets, always a delicate task for some reason.

We drove in from the airport in the most bouncy bus I have ever experienced, together with the yokels on their way into town for some Saturday night fun. The outskirts of the city seemed shabby, but the people looked much healthier than the Muscovites, with good skins. Our hotel room is actually a suite, and would be just the right size for us as an apartment in Ottawa if the immense bathroom were split in two and one half made into a kitchen. Your golf-ball bath plug has proved useful, by the way, for as usual no bath plug is provided.

We had a good dinner in the very luxurious pre-Revolutionary (I imagine) dining room, eaten to the strains of the usual deafening band. We were joined by a nice young man, and were talking with him when our waitress, backed up by the boss-lady, came to throw him out, or rather to remove him to another table, on the grounds that they were keeping these places for an American couple who would be in later. Peter made a big fuss, but it did turn out to be true, for the Americans turned up an hour later. Still, the young Russian could easily have stayed until they came. The Americans were a pleasant middle-aged lawyer and his wife, who were on a twenty-four day tour of the Soviet Union, and I think beginning to look forward to the twenty-fourth day.

Oh! Peter has just come in to report that there are no seats available on the plane on which we had intended to return to Moscow. Of course there was no means of booking in advance from Moscow, as there is the usual lack of communication between one city and another. Peter is hopping mad, for Posol is alone and was loath enough anyway to be left without any officer at the Embassy during Friday, Saturday, and Sunday, and of course tomorrow is bag day. It is now noon, and we cannot leave the hotel, for we have to hang around in the hope of talking someone into assigning us places on the plane. I hope we do not have to leave without seeing the town at all.

After taking leave of our American companions last night we took a stroll in a sort of unkempt park between the hotel and the sea. I experienced for the first time the way it feels when you know you are being followed, for we spotted a creepy character lurking behind bushes wherever we went. Just to tease him, we once doubled back abruptly, whereupon he attempted to conceal himself behind a much too narrow tree trunk. As we passed him in his hiding place we wished him a good evening, to which greeting he did not reply. I suppose the poor fellow was just doing his job, but it was an eerie experience on a dark night. Perhaps such precautions are viewed as necessary, given that Odessa is a seaport. I know that our service attachés expect to be followed constantly when they travel outside Moscow.

Back in Moscow, May 18th

I had just written the above paragraph when Peter bustled in and told me to start packing! There were no places available on the evening flight we had intended to take, nor could they guarantee us places on the plane leaving early the next morning. Anyway, if Peter were even half a day late returning to the Embassy, that would probably put an end to all weekend trips for all members of staff. So there was nothing for it but to seize the only available seats on the plane that was to leave at 2:00 p.m. We would have to drive straight to the airport as soon as we had received confirmation of the booking. There was not even time to make a tour of the town by taxi on the way to the airport. Well, so much for Odessa. But the Kiev part of the trip was enjoyable and memorable.

Many thanks for letters from all three of you. Liz, June 25th sounds a more likely date for the degree-taking ceremony, but I can't say yes or no until we see how our timetable is working out. Can we make arrangements to participate in the event if we give about ten days' notice?

I have decided to fly together with Peter to Copenhagen on the TU–104, and to continue to London (without Peter) on the same plane. This will be on Saturday 30 May. There is just too much to be done in Moscow to allow me to leave any earlier. The plane is due to arrive in London about lunchtime, but Soviet flights are always unpredictable as regards timing.

Sorry that this is all so disjointed. We have a very busy week ahead of us, and my mind keeps flitting from one subject to another. (I would be hopeless as an office worker.)

I probably won't write to you next week, as I shall be arriving on the postman's heels. We are *so* happy to be coming.

Much love,

Nao.

＊〜　〜＊

Moscow
24 May 1959

My dear Parents,

It is a bit odd to write to you when I am to see you so soon, but I do want to say how grateful I am to you for opening the Zimanage to our invasion and for helping in other ways with our holiday in June. I am looking forward to being at 10 Eton Road; it's a place where I never fail to enjoy myself.

We are off on Saturday morning on the TU–104 to Copenhagen. I still don't like the airplane, after what I have been told of it, but it does happen to be the only suitable flight on that day. Na and I part company at Copenhagen; I will spend the weekend in Hamburg, where I've not been, then pick up the car in Düsseldorf and get to London as fast as I can after that.

The week has been a mad one. We had a lunch on Tuesday for the departing Indian first secretary Ahudja, quite successful as Moscow parties go, and on Friday evening we gave a great buffet dinner. This will be the last ever, for when we get back at the end of June our splendid living room will have been made into an office, and we must skulk in the back corner of the flat, where you slept when you were here.

The Robertis were at the dinner, Paola as mad as ever but amusing withal. The remaining guests were a mixed bag; among them were some American students attending the university here and a Canadian portrait photographer who is trying to take a picture of Khrushchev. No dice so far. Na says the buffet party was a success. I guess it was, but I was in no mood to appreciate it because I had foolishly drunk a dry martini on top of a TABT injection, and felt as though I had the Black Death. In addition to all this, we have also helped to look after the Bishop of Fulham by dining him and taking him to see the Moiseev dancers, whom he greatly admired.

You will be happy to know that I've been promoted, a tribute more to age than talent. But it puts my salary well over the $6,000 mark, which is not princely but should enable us to avoid the penury in which we lived last time in Ottawa. (Naomi reminds me that her annual salary at Carleton remained at $1,600 until she left for financial reasons to become a Civil Service clerk at $2,000 per year. Thanks to the intervention of Hilda Gifford, Carleton later wooed her back by offering her the same sum. My own annual salary in Ottawa was in the $4,000 range.)

Love to you both and to Liz. See you in a little over a week.

Peter

P.S. My promotion is only within the service. My local rank is still Second Secretary.

～

Moscow

4 July 1959

My dear Ma, Pa and Liz,

It is largely owing to the efforts of you three that the main purpose of our month in England was achieved. I am most grateful. My Mother has never before gone on a holiday from which she did not want to return home after a day or two; this time she left England with obvious reluctance, and perhaps has it in mind to come back sometime. These are better results than I had dreamed of, and so much of the success was due to you.

I have also to thank Pa for a most generous birthday present. With your approval, Pa, I think I shall combine it with a similar amount received from my Mother and will buy an electric shaver, which is really a necessary piece of equipment in this wretched two-shaves-a-day life.

Our return trip was not uneventful. The TU–104 was to have left Brussels at about 1300 on Monday. As always, it was late. First they told us it would depart at 1500, and kept us sitting until that time without lunch, then they said 1700, and gave us lunch in the rather dreary airport restaurant; finally they declared that it would not leave until eight o'clock the next morning, and meanwhile we would be taken into town. This meant all the weary business of getting bags off the plane and submitting them to customs inspection, and being prepared to get up at 5:30 a.m. the next day. But the delay was not all bad, for we enjoyed a pleasant, if short, evening wandering about Brussels, which I like better at each time of viewing.

The ostensible reason for the delay was bad weather in Moscow, but I have since learned that the weather was perfect, and that a more probable cause was the arrival of old Emperor Haile Selassie, for whom the Russians had closed the airport. Anyway, the Yaldens were there to meet us and to give us dinner, and the Posol showed the expected annoyance at my late return.

Nao wonders whether she should stay away from the TU–104 in future if she is not to jinx every flight. Granted, her experience on the flight at the end of May affected only the two Western passengers, herself and the *News Chronicle* man. The docile Russian passengers had been re-loaded at Copenhagen, so what was the point of delaying takeoff until the pre-announced departure time? Someone saved for us James Cameron's report of the incident in the *News Chronicle*. He wrote, "I inquired for my flight and was told that it had left, unannounced, and with all my baggage. When I protested that they might let a chap know when the plane was leaving, the man said sombrely: 'It makes enough *noise* doesn't it?'" Cameron made a good and comic story out of the incident, but Nao says that he was thoroughly rattled at the time, for he had left his briefcase in the passenger seat, and it contained all his notes on his completed assignment in India and Russia. Pretty rash of him to let it out of his hands, Nao thought.

On Wednesday we celebrated our National Day with the usual dull cocktail party, though somewhat improved over other years because we used the garden as well as the Ambassador's flat. Mikoyan came, and Kosygin, a good enough catch, considering that Khrushchev no longer attends National Day parties.

Thank you all many times over. I shall write more before long, but just now the Ambassador is on a trip to remote parts of Siberia, and I'm supposed to be minding the shop. Max is also absent from the office all day, accompanying a delegation, so there is plenty to do. Most of this morning, for example, was spent wringing 50,000 roubles out of the Foreign Languages Publishing House for a Canadian author whose books had been published here.

Best love to you all,

Peter

❦

Moscow
5 July 1959

My dear Ma, Pa and Liz,

Thank you for all you did to make the holiday such a success. We both feel more than satisfied, and we know that you were in great part responsible for Mother Roberts' enjoyment of her treat. In addition to all the outings you helped us plan for her, you provided excellent meals, and I have never seen the house looking finer. We came back to Moscow perfectly content with our holiday and relaxed enough to be able to look forward with some pleasure to our final three months here.

The Yaldens met us and fed us — a day later than expected, as Peter has explained in his letter. The only bad news they had to report is that my deep-freeze had broken down while I was away, and as this was not discovered for three days most of the contents had spoiled. Janice retrieved what she could, but there is quite a big loss. The good news is that we still have our sitting room, though it may be taken from us any day now.

I am enjoying being my own cook, and once I catch up on domestic tasks I ought not to be too busy, for the Embassy cleaner is going to "do" for me eleven hours a week. Last week, however, was a bit frantic, what with our National Day, and fresh food stocks to lay in, and holiday laundry to be done, not to mention trying to create some order in Nina's rather sordid kitchen. I had a gala dinner to prepare last night for us and the Yaldens, in celebration of Peter's birthday, but there are no parties anticipated *chez nous* for a while, so I shall be able to calm down next week.

In addition to our own National Day, we have celebrated this week the American Day of Independence and the Royal Wedding in Belgium. Now

I have displayed my three party frocks and hats, so I hope there is not another grand party for a while.

We had a telegram from Calgary to tell us that Mother Roberts had arrived safely. Thanks for looking after her on her last day, Ma, and for seeing her off at the airport. Considering how long we ourselves were delayed, we might just as well have stayed over an extra day in order to see her off in person. Aeroflot (through Sabena) put us up in the Hotel Cecil; do you know it?

Thanks again for the lovely holiday. Love to you all,

Nao.

P.S. Max appears quite recognizably on the front page of *Pravda* this morning. He is the Canadian delegate to the Housing Committee of the European Economic Commission.

⸻ ⁓ ⸻

Moscow
15 July 1959

My dear Parents and Liz,

How are you all? This won't be a long letter, but I wanted to describe to you while it was fresh in my mind the Kremlin reception we recently attended.

The invitation was sent "By command of His Imperial Majesty Haile Selassie 1st Emperor of Ethiopia." The Ambassador of Ethiopia requested the attendance of The Chargé d'Affaires of Canada and Mrs P.M. Roberts at a reception to be given by his Imperial Majesty at the Kremlin Palace "in honour of His Excellency K.E. Voroshilov President of the Presidium of the Supreme Soviet of the U.S.S.R." (Peter was Chargé while the Ambassador was away in Siberia; Posol would not have left Moscow if he had known in advance that he would miss this event.)

The Emperor, a tiny sorrowful-looking figure, had brought one of his daughters as a companion. Once the receiving line had disbanded, the Big Boys as usual congregated behind the laden food and drinks table, pretty well ignoring their host. Worse still, poor Miss Selassie was abandoned in a space in the middle of the reception room, no one speaking to her but many staring at her. I was very tempted to do the decent thing by approaching her in order to start a conversation, but I knew that protocol forbade such a thing and that I would bring disgrace upon Peter, probably one of the most junior officers present. So I tried to send waves of sympathy in her direction. British colleagues told me that she is a recent Oxford graduate (Somerville, I think). I hope that she had some happy years there, for her life now cannot be much fun, to judge from what we witnessed.

Once the Big Boys and the principal guests and their hosts had departed, the minor Soviet guests swarmed around the food table and carried off all that was fit to eat, plus the flowers snatched from their vases. I like it when that happens. It seems a very practical and natural way to take advantage of the opportunity offered.

That's all for now.

Much love,

Nao.

⸺ ⸺

Moscow

27 July 1959

My dear Ma, Pa and Liz,

The time is whizzing past, with nothing much done to boast about. We spent one glorious evening after work at one of Moscow's pleasant beaches, and another afternoon (Saturday) at the same place, and we have attended reluctantly a couple of small dinner parties, and that's about all since last week.

At one of the dinner parties the guests included a quite young German couple. After dinner the host introduced party games, which I don't mind at all (they provide a welcome break from making conversation), though Peter is not keen. But we both were amused this time, for the German guest had a maniacal laugh, which he exercised during the games at the slightest provocation, and his wife kept scolding him, saying, "Lach doch nicht so 'hee-hee-hee.'" It seemed not to bother him at all to be publicly rebuked in this way.

The other dinner party was given by a British colleague for Walter Laqueur and his wife. As you undoubtedly know, he is the editor of *Soviet Survey*, and writes books about Communism in the Middle East, and contributes to *International Affairs*. He says he has met Pa. They are a pleasant couple. She managed to see her mother and brother for the first time since 1936, at which time they all left Germany, some of the family going to Russia and others (including Mrs Laqueur) to Palestine.

On Friday we attended (by invitation) the opening of the famous American Exhibition, and heard Nixon's excellent speech. (In fact, I saw him at rather too close quarters, for I happened to be standing in the way when his entourage swept by, and his security men almost crushed me against a wall.) The Russians are of course panting to get into the Exhibition, but tickets are hard to come by and are being distributed to the deserving through various official organizations (as tickets for most events are). The undeserving are very fed up about this. Nevertheless, several thousand a day do see the display, and are impressed. It is all in fact quite modest, and the controversial "model home" is a simple affair, not at all misleading as an example of a "worker's" house. All the same, the house and the rest look pretty tempting to the honest Soviet citizen.

The Trade Delegation has not yet arrived. I don't know if they will still come. The Seaborns are expected the second week of August.

Much love,

Nao.

Moscow

2 August 1959

My dear Ma, Pa and Liz,

We've both got the can't-wait-to-leave feeling, with less than two months left here, and our belongings to be on their way in three weeks.

Our pleasant travel times were all knocked for six a couple of weeks ago when somebody in Ottawa conceived the idea of having me spend a week in Warsaw on the way home. The reason for this is that I am to work on Eastern European affairs when I am back in Ottawa. This means probably that we shall leave Moscow by air on September 26 or thereabouts and get to London, via Warsaw and Amsterdam, about October 5. Do let us know if you are likely to be away at that time, because any time that I spend in London will be annual leave, and there will be no point in taking it if you are not there. (If we had come, as planned, on the *Baltika*, our four or five days in London would have been a legitimate stopover. When we travel by air we have to work out an itinerary that will provide no more than one day's stopover in London.)

The best thing to occur in Moscow for a long time is the arrival of the Australians. The advance party of a Chargé, a Second Secretary, and a stenographer turned up a few days ago. I wish they had come sooner, for they are the first foreign diplomats we've known in Moscow with whom we can get along much as we do with Canadian colleagues. We entertained them in a preliminary way yesterday by taking the whole gang to a splendid swimming hole we have found, about twenty-five miles to the west, and there serving a picnic lunch. They were cowardly about getting into the cold water of the Moscow River (cold by Aussie standards, I suppose, though very warm by Rocky Mountain standards), but once in the water they all proved themselves magnificent swimmers. They were not cowardly when it came to the martinis and a couple of bottles of my best Graves. I ingratiated myself with the Chargé's wife by catching six little fish in a plastic bag (a throwback to remote childhood, fishing in the Lethbridge irrigation canal) and carrying them home for her in a wine bottle. She intended to put them in among other little, but more exotic, specimens in her fish bowl.

Here all is in flux. Max Yalden and I sat down for half a day last week and designed a daring scheme, which involves almost everybody in a change of accommodation.. It puts some people in flats smaller than they now have, but it means that this, our present flat, will remain intact indefinitely, and, more importantly, that all the new staff about to arrive will be housed in some kind of flat and not in a hotel. We bore this plan to the Posol, who had been saying for at least a year that he would consider nothing of the sort, and he agreed to it almost at once. It will all happen with a crash when we leave; Yaldens will take over this flat, and their move will be followed by a whole series of others. Can you picture it? Hundreds of Canadians hauling their furniture and wine cellars across Moscow. Posol himself may be moving too. He is probably going to Canada in October to receive an honorary degree from McGill and after that I cannot really imagine that Norman Robertson will send him back here. He has had over three years here, and is keen to get out.

Did you know a man called de Margerie who was at the French Embassy in London? (Yes, Nao reminds me that you do know him.) He is now posted to the Embassy in Moscow, and he invited us to dinner, much to our surprise, for the French usually treat the Canadians as though we belonged to the FLN. It was the best meal we have yet eaten in Moscow, cooked by Madame herself, mostly from local products. Aside from the food, though, the evening was a bit dull, especially the last hour, which was taken up by an acrimonious dispute between the new British Third Secretary and his wife: "Darling, do let's stop being personal and be logical for a minute." Before this exchange, he had explained to us how he had got a first at Oxford, and how his wife certainly would have got a first had he not distracted her with courting. She, when her turn came, lectured Naomi and me on the religious inspiration available to us through a close study of English cathedrals.

Next weekend, if all is well we will go to Riga, just to have a look and to have a swim at the famous beach. It is the only Soviet Baltic city that is open to foreigners, but it is said to be the most attractive of the three. I'm sure it will be a sad place, like Lvov and the other non-Russian cities of the west and south.

Love to you all. We are looking forward to seeing you, come October.
Peter

P.S. from Naomi: No letter from me this week, as I am writing at length to P's family, but thanks, Ma, for a lovely long and funny letter.

Moscow
10 August 1959

My dear Parents and Liz,

Thanks for nice long letters from Ma and from Liz. So sorry, Liz, that the cottage was damp and the landlady unwilling, and I hope that you managed to avoid catching colds and that you enjoyed the birdwatching. At least the walks along the sands were enjoyable.

Speaking of which, we spent an hour last weekend on the fine sands of the beach at Riga. I did paddle in the Baltic Sea, but did not go so far as to swim in the ocean — too cold. Riga itself must once have been an attractive city, but is now a rather sorry sight, very shabby and rundown. It has some beautiful parks and wooded areas, and a very handsome river, so the *natural* parts are still quite fine. There are many handsome houses still standing on the outskirts, which were of course formerly "one-family dwellings" but are now split up into apartments. Even so, the superficial effect is still one of real houses with real gardens attached. Similarly, the buildings in the shopping areas are so reminiscent of those in other European cities — German or Austrian especially — that one keeps expecting to see bright displays of goods in the windows and gay restaurants and cafés, and it comes as a shock as one approaches to see only another display of the drab goods that are now so familiar, and yet another fly-blown, sad *stolovaya*.

We had quite an interesting ride in a taxi driven by a local of the old days, a Latvian who had been deported to the East together with so many of his fellow-countrymen, but who had since been allowed to return. He made few comments, but his smile and his ironically raised eyebrow told us pretty well what he felt about conditions today. Another interesting encounter was with an attractive young Russian engineer, aged about twenty. We talked with him for about three hours over dinner, and though he was very well versed in the party line he did not have an absolutely closed mind.

It took us two and a half hours each way to fly to and from Riga, and that will be our last trip from Moscow. The next holiday will be in the Western world.

And speaking of travel, there have been yet further revisions regarding our departure, owing to changes in the airline timetables. As things now stand, we leave *Mockba* for Warsaw on Saturday 26 September, leave

Warsaw for Paris on Saturday 3 October, stay in Paris for the nights of 3 and 4 October, leave for London on Monday 5 October in the evening. That gives us Tuesday, Wednesday, and Thursday in London; we sail on Friday. Our home leave has been approved, so we will travel more or less straight from Montreal to Lethbridge, though possibly delaying a couple of days in order to rescue the car from its C.P.R. storage in Montreal and to place it somewhere cheaper.

Will you all be in London October 5th to 9th? And please may we stay at 10 Eton Road if you have room for us? (We will be on leave, not on Government time.) We will not burden you with a vast amount of baggage, for we are sending all but our allotted forty-four pounds of air baggage by sea to Canada under the wing of Don Knox (our friend the Naval Attaché, remember?). We need to have our sea baggage all packed up by August 25th, a whole month before we leave. (Memories of sending the school trunks by Carter Paterson weeks before the start of term....)

You will be glad to learn that our two sofas and two wing chairs have been re-upholstered, as have also all the dining-room chairs. And we have a new carpet in the dining room and another in your late bedroom, and five new lamps. After we have left, the Yaldens will move into this apartment, bringing nearly all the furniture from their present flat, so most of our furniture will be distributed among the flats intended for new staff members. What a gorgeous muddle it is going to be, and how lucky that we won't be here to share in it.

Lots of love from us both,

N.

———

Moscow

17 August 1959

My dear Ma and Pa (also Liz),

Thanks for your fine letter, Ma. I enjoyed all your stories about the American Cousins. Are these the same people who wondered whether there are sewers in London?

I am in a rush just now because tomorrow is our monster party to welcome the Seaborns (he is our new Counsellor) and Janice and I are about to make baby pizza for 102 guests. Blair and Carol Seaborn will be splendid colleagues; we knew them a little in Ottawa, and they have two of the best-behaved children you could ever hope to meet. As a matter of fact, you (parents) may remember meeting Blair's brother the Dean of the Cathedral in Quebec City while you were visiting us at Bishop's University.

It was thanks to his letter of introduction that we were invited by the Ottawa Seaborns during our early days in that city.

What with the arrival of the Seaborns last week, and the party tomorrow, and all the packing to be done, this is a busy period. But September should be pleasantly free and unencumbered, and you may hope for a better letter from me.

The drama critic of the *Globe and Mail*, Herbie Whittaker, is now in Moscow and will shortly be coming to London. He is an agreeable, stimulating companion, even if his capacity to stay up late far exceeds ours. The Yaldens twice entertained him at dinner; as former Toronto people they are old fans. He is highly regarded in the theatre world and is considered to be one of the best drama critics in Canada.

It is pizza preparation time, so forgive me if I send just this brief note. Lots of love,

N.

———

Moscow
24 August 1959

My dear Ma, Pa, and Liz,

Only a tiny note from Ma to Peter to answer this week; I find that I am out of touch with your movements and plans. Perhaps today's bag will bring me up to date.

I have no special wishes as regards our brief stay in England in October, except that I should like to make a day trip to Oxford in order to see our dear Wub, since one never knows that it may not be the last time.

Last Tuesday we gave our mammoth cocktail party for the Seaborns; at least it was to have been mammoth, but only fifty-five of the invited 102 guests turned up. Those who did come appeared to enjoy themselves, however, so all is well.

On Saturday we went again to the American Exhibition. The Exhibition itself is a shambles now (I never did think it was all that impressive, as a matter of fact, even when it was new and clean, though Peter disagrees). However, it has become a very lively place where views are aired and political subjects discussed. The American guides (mostly undergraduates or post-graduate students, all fluently Russian-speaking) have groups of Soviet citizens around them asking questions about America and sometimes heckling them. On the whole the Russians are polite and good-natured while discussing matters of interest, and the crowd sometimes turns on the heckler in support of the guide. There were some particularly lively debates and arguments taking place in the modern art pavilion. The Russians mostly argued with one another rather than with the guide, and sometimes became quite heated in their championship or condemnation of the pictures. (I thought most of the pictures were pretty awful, to tell you the truth.) The most successful feature of the Exhibition is the fact that it has provided an opportunity for open speech and discussion.

We are having super late-summer weather, hot during the day and cool at night. A whole lot of open-air vegetable stalls have opened up, under red and white awnings, several local buildings have had a facelift, and altogether I have never seen Moscow looking so winsome.

Much love to you all,

Nao.

Moscow

30 August 1959

My dear Ma, Pa, Liz,

The week has consisted of one cocktail party after another, to say goodbye to this person and hello to that person. Several of the goodbyes were for Alan Urwick, who, as I expect you remember, kindly invited the parents to dinner during their visit. He has been a good friend since early days in Moscow.

This is the turnover season in most of the Western embassies. The service attachés go to extreme lengths in their reception of newcomers. Our new Military Attaché and his wife arrived on Tuesday and they were presented at a champagne party to the Embassy staff on Wednesday. They were invited to lunch on Thursday to meet twenty of the service attachés of the Western diplomatic corps, and on the following evening they were entertained at a party for the twenty lunch guests (again) plus the remainder of the Western service attachés. Next week the Attaché's wife on her own is to be presented to all the wives of the service attachés. As fellow-Canadians, we are invited to these parties too. Next week the new Naval Attaché and his wife arrive, and we go through the whole business again. At the all-women functions I will have the chance to observe some of the service wives from countries where English and the other more familiar Western languages are not spoken. Poor lost souls, what a horrible strain for them to sit through these social events nodding and smiling and nibbling on snacks, understanding little or nothing of what is spoken.

Have you heard of the Oxford students who are travelling in the Soviet Union in a former London bus? We had four of them to a late supper on Tuesday. They arrived in their bus, leaving it parked outside the Embassy, to the delight of the neighbours. Before they left, they generously took us for a ride in the bus. I do hope they get home safely; it all seems pretty hazardous.

Next Friday Peter and Blair will leave on their trip to Tbilisi, Yerevan, Batumi, and Sukhumi, from which they do not return until Sunday 13 September. Jacques Montpetit (Peter's replacement) is expected on September 12th, and the Ambassador goes to Canada on leave on the 16th. On 25 September Peter and I leave Moscow for Vilnius, which (like Yerevan) has just been opened to foreigners. On 27 September we continue to Warsaw and remain there a full week. On Saturday 3 October we fly to Paris. As you already know, we expect to fly from Paris to London late on Monday 5 October. What a lot of travelling and new places to see.

Quite suddenly cool weather has come to Moscow and we are sitting huddled over our electric radiator with windows firmly shut. I find that the skirts of my winter clothes need to be shortened *again*. I was not sufficiently bold last year.

No more now. Perhaps my letters will be more interesting after I have visited some new places.

Much love, Nao.

P.S. We cannot break our journey in Vilnius after all, for we are not able to book onward transportation in advance (the usual story), and we might be stuck there for days. Oh, bother. I had really wanted to get a glimpse of Lithuania.

◆━━◆

Moscow
1 September 1959

My dear Liz.

This one is for you and you only. It is a sad little tale concerning someone you have met. Please don't share it.

You must have heard us speak of the ever-present threat of "entrapment," but we have never told you of an actual incident. The reason for this is that when a member of the staff of any Embassy leaves in a hurry the matter is kept private and usually only immediate colleagues know about it, and they don't tell. What is likely to happen is that the victim of the entrapment reports the circumstances to the head of mission and is discreetly whisked away before he or she can become further embroiled. (Of course, if the matter is *not* reported, the danger escalates and the victim becomes vulnerable to blackmail. In that case we won't know anything about it until and unless that person is discovered acting improperly and is prosecuted.)

However, a reported incident has occurred that has become public knowledge (though on a limited scale, I hope).

Do you remember telling us how surprised you were when a certain junior service attaché who was travelling with you on the *Baltika* produced upon arrival in Leningrad a wife and two little girls who were also on board? Like all the other young single passengers who had enjoyed one another's company on the voyage, you had assumed that this playmate was travelling alone.

Well, it seems that this pattern of behaviour continued, i.e., that the wife was pretty much excluded or ignored by her husband.

During the summer the senior service attaché of that foreign mission and his wife were away on home leave. The Soviet driver assigned to him was now at the disposal of the junior attaché, who, in the slack summer season, had little need of his services and therefore authorized the driver to take the wife and children to the beach for occasional excursions. Not willing to miss an opportunity for mischief, the true bosses of the driver instructed him to try to win the affections of the wife (to what immediate end I don't know). But the poor wife turned the tables on the lot of them by responding enthusiastically to the driver's sweet words and offering to leave her husband and to settle down with the driver in the Soviet Union. The driver already had a family of his own and was horrified by this turn of events. Result: the junior attaché was immediately sent home from his posting in disgrace. One hates to think of the recriminations in that family, though in the opinion of many the husband was to blame for what happened. His poor duped wife had longed only for attention and affection — or so we suppose. It was probably a mistake to post that particular family to Moscow, with all its built-in tensions.

The only reason that I know all this is that the senior attaché was called back to Moscow at short notice, having lost both his assistant and his driver, and was so angry with his assistant that he let the story become public.

You will be receiving a more general letter from me this week, addressed to you and the parents. For now, goodbye and much love,

Nao.

Moscow
6 September 1959

My dear Ma, Pa and Liz,

Thanks to Ma and Liz for their good letters.

As I told you in my P.S. last week, our trip to Vilnius is OFF, alas, but Peter left with Blair on Friday evening, heading south. We have had one phone call from our husbands and are expecting another tonight or tomorrow. By the time that P. comes back there will be less than two weeks to spend in Moscow, and almost every evening is already booked.

We attended a variety of parties last week, nearly all farewell occasions in honour of someone or other. We ourselves entertained four of our office staff to lunch at the Praga restaurant, which as you may remember is at Arbat Square. We had *syomka* (salted salmon) and Chicken Kiev and salad and ice cream and Turkish coffee and vodka and Georgian wine, and it wasn't at all bad, in fact pretty good.

Last night I went to one more *Narodni Khor* (popular song and dance), this time performed by a troupe from Omsk. It was all very much in the Soviet-realism mode and message-laden, one song in particular celebrating the glory of corn grown in Siberia. I had to leave at halftime in order to welcome some colleagues from Paris who are at present on holiday in the S.U., and I was not really sorry to miss the second half. A little of the Russian folk music goes a long way, I find.

This evening Gaitskill and Bevan spoke for thirty minutes on Soviet T.V. I had not realized how very Welsh Bevan sounds; rather pleasant.

Do you suppose I can safely go and run a bath, or will the phone ring from Tbilisi as soon as I get into the water? I think I'll risk it anyway.

Much love, Nao.

⌒⌒

Moscow
14 September 1959

My dear Liz, and Parents if they can be reached,

Ma's card from Edinburgh arrived a couple of hours ago. Glad to hear that we will overlap in Paris. Peter's jaw dropped slightly at the news, but he rallied quickly and professed himself not in the least horrified ... Perhaps we will all travel back to London together, though you may need to leave before we do, in order to find time to draw breath between your return and our arrival.

Liz, will you be able to take some time off work on the 7th or 8th so that we can do things together?

Peter returned yesterday from his nine-day trip with Blair. They had quite a good time but were both delighted when it was over. P. lost some weight and looks generally healthier in spite of the poor food. The exercise and open air did him good.

I was madly busy while he was away and achieved a lot. Now we have a week and a half of non-stop parties ahead of us, but it doesn't matter, as the new Third Secretary has arrived and there is very little work for P. to do.

Much love,

N.

✦

On board the *Empress of Britain*
10 October 1959

My dear Liz,

I promised that I would send you an account of our Warsaw experience, as you were not present when we were telling the parents about that week. Also, I am glad to have a record of the events for my own interest. So here goes.

Ideally, we would have liked to stay anonymously in a hotel, in order to recover from all the social activities of the last weeks in Moscow. But that does not happen among colleagues. The Ambassador had arranged for us to stay at the home of one of his senior officers; this colleague and his wife provided us with excellent quarters and were entirely correct and hospitable in their behaviour toward us, but we felt that we were intruding upon them and it was not a comfortable situation.

Peter was introduced to the local political scene, and no doubt learned a lot, but he will have to tell you about that himself.

Together one day we visited the Old Town, which has been rebuilt and restored according to the records of the destroyed original. I believe there are differences of opinion as to whether this morale-building exercise ought to have taken priority over the creation of new homes for the struggling population. Thirteen years after the Germans were driven out by the Russians (following the brave but failed Warsaw uprising, which the Soviet forces watched from the far side of the river) there is still much evidence of the devastation suffered during the Occupation. In fact it is said that about eighty-five percent of the city lay in ruins by the end of the war in Europe.

The Ambassador invited us to dinner one night, together with other officers from the Embassy, and it was strange to see the table laid with the same pattern of china, glass, and silverware with which we had become so familiar during the many occasions when we sat at our own Posol's table.

Fortunately we had one good friend on the Embassy staff, a junior officer called Peter Scott (son of Frank Scott, one of Canada's best-known poets, and of his artist wife, Marian Scott, and incidentally nephew of one of our Bishop's colleagues, Eldon Scott). Peter's wife Maylie (a very attractive American) had worked with me for a short time at the Circulation Desk of the Library at Carleton College, and the four of us had entertained one another a few times in Ottawa. Peter and Maylie obtained from the Ambassador permission to make a short trip by car to Krakow, taking us with them, plus their very new baby girl.

This was the highlight of the week for us; just being in their company was fun. During a visit to the Krakow museum the woman assigned to be the personal guide of the Canadian visitors made a point of indicating where the famous tapestries ought to be hanging but were not. They are in fact in Quebec City, having been spirited to Canada for safe-keeping in advance of the German occupation. (It is a matter of friction between our two countries because the Quebec government refuses to return them to what has become a "Godless country." Ask Pa to tell you the story of how he asked Premier Duplessis about the Polish Treasures, and was allowed to view them, accompanied by an armed guard.)

I in fact was not present while the others visited the museum. I had been left in charge of the sleeping child in the car. Maylie is still nursing her baby, and wouldn't you know it, the baby woke up (hungry, of course) and began to wail, louder and ever louder. Presently a crowd of inquisitive Polish women surrounded the car, and it was not hard to interpret their indignant comments as instructions to me to nurse the baby. I was forced to confess (in Russian and by gesture) that 1) I was not the mother and 2) I therefore had no milk. They roared with laughter at my discomfiture. When the others returned they laughed too. I did not find it so funny.

It was our intention the following day to drive back to Warsaw in good time to collect our possessions and to pay our respects to our hosts before leaving. But we ran into trouble. The highway between these two major cities is much of it rough-surfaced and single-lane, and we were unlucky enough to find ourselves behind a horse-drawn farmer's cart, which we had no choice but to follow at cart-horse speed. We were so delayed by these circumstances that all we could do when we reached Warsaw was to dash upstairs and pack our things, apologize profusely to our hostess, then drive off with the Scotts to the airport. The hostess had prepared a beautiful tea for us, which we did not have time to sample, and she had every reason to think us ill-mannered guests. It was a poor end to an otherwise fine excursion.

I will be writing to Ma and Pa later today, so do ask to see their letter and to read my account of life on shipboard.

I hope you will plan to come and stay with us in Ottawa soon. Goodness knows what accommodation we will find, but you know we will have at least a camp bed for you to sleep on.

Thanks for your many services during our first European posting, and much love from

Nao.

—⁓—

Greenock
Empress of Britain
10 October 1959

My dear Ma and Pa,

All is well with us. We have a smashing cabin, complete with bath, shower, handbasin, and lav., and all the public rooms are comfortable and pleasant. The tourist class rooms equally so, as far as I have been able to observe, and it seems rather unnecessary for the Canadian Government to put us up in this super-luxury, but we are not complaining. Unless we experience very rough weather, this should be an agreeable and restful week.

The only travelling companion whose name we recognize is His Grace the Archbishop of York. We observe that there is a Mrs Taylor of Lennoxville among the tourist class passengers, but we don't think it is my old friend Jennifer of Bishop's University.

Thank you so much for letting us stay, and I am sorry that we saw so little of you both during that time. We always try to get too much done while we are in London. But I am pleased with all the purchases I made on my two shopping expeditions, and we will have some nice gifts to present to the Lethbridge folk. I forgot to tell Pa that the suit I was wearing when we left was my Birthday Suit, paid for out of his birthday ten pounds and Mother Roberts's birthday five pounds combined. So thank you, Pa and Mrs R.

Now I must go and find the launderette on Deck C and the hairdresser on Deck B.

Goodbye, and lots of love to you both.

Ever,

Nao.

—⁓—

Greenock
Empress of Britain
10 October 1959

My dear Parents,

You were very kind to let us stay, especially as you preceded us by only one hour. Isn't it a pity that every time we see you we are in a mad tear of packing or unpacking, and I don't find time to savour the full pleasure of life at 10 Eton Road.

We are parked at Greenock at the moment, taking on board about eight passengers and adding a full day to the length of the voyage. However, the ship is good, our cabin splendid, and our fellow-passengers dull (except perhaps for the Archbishop of York). We share a table with the First Officer and a Toronto man and wife, he just retired from having managed Canada's largest slaughterhouse. Charming conversation with the fried kidneys.

We both send our love to you and Liz, and our thanks for a nice conclusion to our first European tour of duty.

Affectionately,

Peter

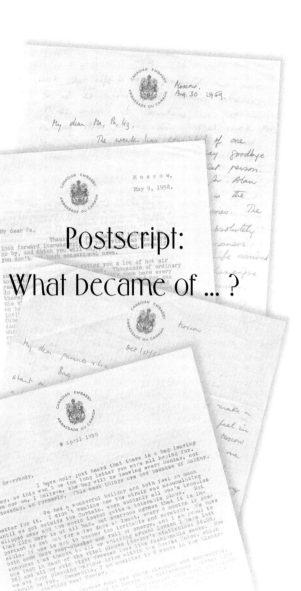

Postscript:
What became of ... ?

THE CORRESPONDENTS

NAOMI ROBERTS returned to Ottawa with her husband after the Moscow posting, and briefly resumed her position as a library assistant at Carleton University, but soon left it in order to take up domestic duties as the mother of a daughter and a son. In 1962 she and the small children accompanied Peter Roberts when he was posted to Hong Kong, then to Washington, D.C., and finally to Brussels, where he spent a year at Canada's mission to NATO. The social obligations of the wife of a mid-level embassy officer in Washington proved less demanding than those Naomi had experienced in Moscow; this allowed her the freedom to attend classes at an American university, where she earned a Master's degree in Library Science, a qualification that was to prove a valuable asset.

In 1970 the family returned to Ottawa, where Peter Roberts took up new duties, and in 1971 Naomi began work as a librarian with the Ottawa Board of Education. Two years later she became a member of the professional library staff at Carleton University, where she occupied a variety of positions in the field of reference and collection-building until her retirement in 1995.

PETER M. ROBERTS continued through the ranks of External Affairs, with postings in Hong Kong, Saigon, and Washington, D.C. A posting to NATO Brussels in 1969 was interrupted after one year by an invitation from the Prime Minister's Office for Peter to return to Ottawa as assistant press secretary, soon to become press secretary, to Prime Minister Pierre E. Trudeau. Peter was granted secondment from External Affairs for this purpose. Three years later, in 1973, he returned to the Department and was assigned the short-term function of organizing the logistics of the Commonwealth Heads of Government meeting, which was to take place in Canada that summer. Soon afterwards, Peter was appointed assistant under-secretary responsible for cultural affairs in the Department of the Secretary of State.

Peter returned to the diplomatic life when in 1979 he was appointed ambassador to Romania. He had separated from his wife, and his family remained in Canada. Following his divorce in 1980 he married Glenna Reid (Woolley).

After four years in Bucharest Peter was named Canadian ambassador to the U.S.S.R. He was delighted to make use of his skill in the Russian language once again and to observe the changes then taking place in Soviet affairs. This posting was cut short after two years, however, when Prime Minister Brian Mulroney appointed Peter director of the Canada Council, a position he continued to fill until his retirement in 1989.

Peter maintained a continuing interest in Russia and an affection for its people. He was the founding chairman of the External Advisory Board of the Centre for Research on Canadian-Russian Relations (CRCR) at Carleton University, and long remained a member of the Board.

Peter was granted the Skelton-Clarke fellowship at Queen's University and used this opportunity to prepare a book about the art collector George Costakis, who had been a long-time local employee at the Canadian embassy in Moscow and had become a friend during Peter's first posting there, as is revealed in some of the letters included in the present volume. The resulting book was published by Carleton University Press in 1994 under the title *George Costakis: A Russian Life in Art*.

A book of personal anecdotes that Peter had originally assembled with the sole purpose of sharing them with his family was later published as *Raising Eyebrows: An Undiplomatic Memoir* (Golden Dog Press, 1999).

Meanwhile Peter had become seriously ill with cancer, but continued to write, working with the assistance of his wife Glenna on a book reflecting his experiences in Romania. This work was published posthumously in 2005 by Chestnut Publishing Group under the title *Revenge on Christmas Day: Fact and Fiction in Bucharest*. It is a work of the imagination, its chapters based upon personal knowledge of the regime that ended in 1989.

Peter had also done research on the "Return to the Homeland" campaign. During the 1950s the Soviet authorities had urged former citizens of what had now become Soviet territory to leave their Canadian homes and return to the Soviet Union. Many responded, some accompanied by their Canadian-born children, only to discover that neither they nor their children were permitted to leave the U.S.S.R. At the embassy Peter was contacted by some of these unhappy people who wished to return to Canada, but he could do little to help at that time. These encounters are not reflected in the personal letters of the period, for reports on such a matter would be reserved for confidential dispatches.

As is explained in the Preface to the present volume, Peter Roberts was aware of the likely publication of our "letters home" from the Soviet Union, but he had no hand in the editing of the material.

MURIEL ROBERTS and her daughter MARY ROBERTS left their home in Lethbridge in 1968 and settled in Ottawa, where Mary Roberts worked as a public health nurse with the Ontario government until her retirement in 1984. Mother and daughter travelled together in the 1980s to Bucharest and to Moscow to visit the Ambassador and his wife. At the embassy in Moscow the domestic staff referred to Muriel Roberts as "Mama Posol." Muriel Roberts died in 1996 at the age of 96.

H.D. ZIMAN, after a career in journalism as editorial-writer, war correspondent, literary editor, and special correspondent, retired from the *Daily Telegraph* in 1968 and died in 1983.

Several boxes of his personal papers were accepted by the Bodleian Library in Oxford, where they are held in the western manuscript collections. In addition to the manuscript material (mainly exchanges of letters with contemporaries in the arts, in the military, and in the literary and newspaper world), the Library holds some scrapbooks of newspaper clippings of H.D. Ziman's published work. Among these records are the articles containing his reflections on life in the Soviet Union as he had observed it during his visit to Moscow with his wife in 1958.

JEAN (MACALISTER) ZIMAN assisted her husband by reviewing and commenting on his articles and book reviews and by maintaining order among his business and personal papers. (During the war years she had served as a private secretary in the Public Relations section of Canadian Military Headquarters in London.) Jean Ziman died in 1992.

Their daughter ELIZABETH ZIMAN (also a visitor to Moscow during the Roberts's posting) was a librarian at the Senate House of the University of London throughout her professional life. She died in 2000.

THE CANADIAN COLLEAGUES

MARSHALL A. CROWE left the Department of External Affairs in 1961 in order to become economic advisor to the Canadian Imperial Bank of Commerce. In 1967 he was appointed assistant secretary to the Cabinet and assistant clerk of the Privy Council of Canada. In 1969 he became deputy secretary to the Cabinet. In 1971 he was appointed president of the Canada

Development Corporation, and from 1973 to 1977 he was chairman of the National Energy Board. In 1978 he established M.A. Crowe Consultants, Inc. In 1994, after graduating from the University of Ottawa law school, he was called to the bar of Ontario, and in 1995 was elected a bencher of the Law Society of Upper Canada.

DORIS M. CROWE worked for CBC Radio during the 1960s, and after an extensive tour and many interviews, she wrote and narrated a series of documentaries on life in the Soviet Union. In the 1970s Doris Crowe was public relations director for the Canadian Nurses Association. For the last twenty years of her life she and Marshall Crowe ran a farm near Portland, Ontario, where she was instrumental in introducing the Dexter cow to Canada. Doris Crowe died in 2003.

VICTOR C. MOORE was posted to Karachi from 1960 to 1962, then to The Hague from 1962 to 1965. From 1965 to 1967 he was head of the Canadian Delegation to the International Commission for Supervision and Control in Vietnam. Back in Ottawa, he was advisor to a number of committees, mainly concerning Commonwealth affairs, and in 1968 was appointed High Commissioner to Jamaica. Upon return to Ottawa in 1972 he became director of the Commonwealth Division. From 1976 to 1979 he was High Commissioner to Zambia and Malawi and Ambassador to Mozambique. Himself an army veteran of the Second World War, in 1979 Victor Moore was appointed deputy commandant and director of studies at the National Defence College in Kingston, Ontario. After his retirement in 1983 he and his wife made their home in Kingston, where he died in 2000.

J. BLAIR SEABORN remained a public servant until his retirement in 1989, occupying senior positions in a variety of fields. In 1964–65 he was Canadian Commissioner to the International Commission for Supervision and Control in Vietnam. (In Saigon, incidentally, he was, for a few months, the senior colleague of Peter Roberts, who was on a short-term posting. They have both written on their Vietnam experience in *Canadian Peacekeepers in Indo-China 1954–1973: Recollections*, edited by Arthur E. Blanchette [Golden Dog Press, 2002]). Blair Seaborn was twice head of the Eastern European section of External Affairs, and from 1967 to 1970 head of the Far Eastern

Division. He was then appointed Assistant Deputy Minister (Consumer Affairs) of the Department of Consumer and Corporate Affairs. From 1975 to 1982 he served as Deputy Minister of Environment Canada. In 1982 he was appointed Canadian Chairman of the International Joint Commission, and from 1985 to 1989 he was senior advisor to the Privy Council Office (Intelligence and Security Co-ordinator). After his retirement, he served from 1990 to 1998 as chairman of the Environmental Assessment Panel of the Long-term Management of Nuclear Fuel Waste. He has been in charge of the restoration of Christ Church Cathedral since 1989. Blair Seaborn is a Member of the Order of Canada.

CAROL SEABORN. After the couple's return to Ottawa from the posting in Vietnam, Carol Seaborn worked for twenty-five years (from 1970 to 1995) for the Parliamentary Centre. Here she did research on foreign affairs subjects for parliamentary committees, and she advised Canadian parliamentary delegations on their meetings with foreign parliamentarians both in Canada and abroad. This work took her to the United States, Western Europe, Eastern Europe, and the Middle East.

HOWARD B. SINGLETON was serving at the Canadian embassy in Helsinki when he visited Naomi and Peter Roberts in Moscow in 1958. From 1961 to 1963 he served with the International Control Commission in Laos, then returned to Ottawa, where he held positions in the Department of External Affairs and in the Department of the Secretary of State. From 1972 to 1976 he was Counsellor at the embassy in Washington, then was chargé d'affaires in Beirut for two years. Back in Ottawa, he became director of the Eastern European division, and later of the Western European division. From 1980 to 1983 he was Canada's ambassador to Haiti. The remaining years of his professional life were spent in Ottawa in various departmental positions, including that of Deputy Chief of Protocol from 1988 until his retirement in 1990.

MAXWELL F. YALDEN returned to Ottawa in 1960, and was posted to Paris in 1963. He became Assistant Under-Secretary of State in 1969 and Deputy Minister of Communications in 1973. From 1977 to 1984 he served as Commissioner of Official Languages. He was Canada's ambassador to Belgium

and Luxembourg from 1984 to 1987. From 1987 to 1996 he was Chief Commissioner of the Canadian Human Rights Commission. In 1997 he was
appointed to membership on the United Nations Human Rights Committee. Max Yalden is a Companion of the Order of Canada.

JANICE M. YALDEN entered academic life when the couple settled in
Ottawa in 1969. She taught initially in the Spanish Department at Carleton
University, then in the Department of Linguistics, of which she became
chair in 1978. She was Associate Dean of Arts and Director of the Centre for
Applied Language Studies from 1979 to 1985, and from 1987 to 1992 she
served as Dean of Arts. Janice Yalden is the author of two books and of
many professional reports and articles on language learning and language
teaching. She has also exhibited her paintings (chiefly watercolours) in
Canada and in France.

THE JOURNALIST

MAX FRANKEL continued to work at the *New York Times*. After some major
assignments in the United States and overseas, he served the newspaper as
its executive editor from 1986 to 1994. He received the Pulitzer Prize for
international coverage in 1973.

Max Frankel's autobiography, *The Times of My Life and My Life with The
Times*, was published in 1999 by Random House. This account of his experiences as a reporter and editor embraces many of the major political
events of the era. The story begins with an account of his family's escape
from Nazi Germany in 1939 and his introduction to the life of a refugee in
America. At the time of our acquaintance in Moscow I knew nothing of
this significant chapter in Max Frankel's life.

In 2004 Max Frankel published a second book, *High Noon in the Cold War:
Kennedy, Khrushchev, and the Cuban Missile Crisis* (Ballantine, 2004).

THE FOREIGN OFFICE ASSOCIATES
*(This information has been obtained from published sources,
not from personal knowledge.)*

TED ORCHARD (Edward Eric Orchard) was awarded a C.B.E in 1966. He
spent the years 1953 to 1976 either at the embassy in Moscow or at the Foreign and Commonwealth Office, where he was Director of Research from

1970 to 1976. He later moved into the realm of local government, serving as a member of Waverley Borough Council from 1978 to 1987 and as Mayor of Haslemere in 1987.

— ～ —

KEN SCOTT (later SIR KENNETH) occupied various diplomatic posts during his career in the Foreign Service, including head of chancery in Moscow in 1971. From 1982 to 1985 he was Britain's ambassador to Yugoslavia, after which, from 1985 to 1990, he was assistant private secretary to Queen Elizabeth II.

— ～ —

DEREK THOMAS (later SIR DEREK) was posted abroad to Manila, Sofia, Ottawa, Paris, and Washington, and also occupied senior positions at home. From 1987 to 1989 he was ambassador to Italy, and since then he has been involved in business and in academic life. In his *Who's Who* entry he notes among his recreations "listening to people and music."

— ～ —

JOHN URE (later SIR JOHN) continued his career in the diplomatic service. His assignments included ambassadorial postings to Cuba, Brazil, and Sweden, and a period as assistant under-secretary of state in the Foreign and Commonwealth Office (1981–1984). At the same time (and later) he published several historical books and became an acclaimed travel writer and lecturer. Among his publications is *The Cossacks* (1999). In this book he acknowledges his indebtedness to Sir Patrick Reilly, who as H.M. Ambassador to Moscow took his new third secretary with him in 1957 on a tour of the Ukraine, the Don, and the Caucasus. The writer also pays tribute to Sir Fitzroy Maclean for encouraging his burgeoning interest in the region during Sir Fitzroy's visit to the Soviet Union at that time.

— ～ —

ALAN URWICK (later SIR ALAN) continued his diplomatic career after his Moscow posting, serving in Baghdad, Amman, Washington, Cairo, and Madrid. In 1979 he was appointed Britain's ambassador to Jordan and in 1985 ambassador to Egypt. From 1987 to 1989 he was High Commissioner

to Canada. During the period 1989 to 1995 he served as Serjeant-at-Arms
to the British House of Commons.

THE MOSCOW RESIDENTS

I assume that NINA was sent by *Burobin* to work at some other embassy
after she left our service, for I heard no more of her. I am sorry that I have
no means of telling her of the important role she plays in this book.

GEORGE COSTAKIS continued to work as the local administrator for the
Canadian Embassy and at the same time continued his activities as a passionate and shrewd art collector. Of particular interest to him and to his
many visitors were the works of art created during the brief period known
as the Russian avant-garde, which had begun to flourish just before the
Revolution but which by the mid-1920s was vigorously suppressed, and by
1938 was virtually outlawed.

So successful were George Costakis's efforts to rescue these forgotten
works of art that his collection became well known outside the Soviet
Union. Some of his distinguished visitors published articles in the western
press, and the resulting notoriety brought unwelcome attention from the
authorities. Under the relatively benign rule of Nikita Khrushchev he had
been allowed to travel and lecture abroad and to lend pictures to foreign
galleries for exhibition, but the Brezhnev regime was less accommodating.
He and his family suffered KGB harassment, increased surveillance, and
intimidation. Some works of art were stolen from his apartment, and his
brother's dacha suffered a serious fire, during which paintings by Anatoli
Zverev and others that were stored there mysteriously disappeared. These
hostile acts reduced him to a state of apprehension both for his family and
for his art collection; reluctantly, he eventually sought permission to leave
the Soviet Union to take up residence in Greece (he was in fact a Greek
national, although he had always lived in Russia).

Negotiations took place, as the result of which most members of the
family left the country in 1978. The art collector was allowed to take with
him one-fifth of his valuable collection on condition that he donate the
remainder to the state. He was content to see his treasures accepted for
display in Russian museums, where he had always felt that they belonged.

Official Soviet attitudes toward the formerly despised avant-garde artists gradually changed, and in 1986 George Costakis was invited back to Moscow with full honours to attend the ceremonial opeining of the New Tretyakov Gallery, the centrepiece of which was an exhibition of private collections donated to the Soviet state, among them a selection of works from the Georgii Dionisovich Kostaki collection. The value of his gift to the nation had been recognized and his life's work validated.

George Costakis died in 1990. He and his family had sold some of the works of art he had been allowed to export in 1978, and he had become a wealthy man. But he had long been a sick man, and he had never ceased to pine for the country that he considered his true home.

A full biography of this former employee of the Canadian government, *George Costakis: A Russian Life in Art* (Carleton University Press, 1994), was prepared by Peter Roberts. Parts of the remarkable story are told in George Costakis's own words, transcribed from hours of taped interviews.

An illustrated record of a large part of the collection is provided in the volume entitled *Russian Avant-garde Art: The George Costakis Collection* (Harry M. Abrams, 1981), edited by Angelica Zander Rudenstine. This volume includes introductory texts by S. Frederick Starr and by George Costakis himself.

Additional references to George Costakis and his collection occur in academic journals and in magazine articles.

❦

ANATOLI ZVEREV did not live long enough to experience full official acceptance of his art. Dismissed from art school as a young man, he continued to draw and paint with fervour. He was scorned by the authorities, who regarded him as a parasite without merit, but he had a few admirers who recognized his natural talent. Foremost among these was George Costakis, who became his friend, his patron, and his protector. Thanks largely to George Costakis's connections, Zverev was able to sell some of his pictures, chiefly to foreigners. The meagre income resulting from these sales enabled him to obtain brushes and paints. (Most of his works, mainly gouaches, were painted on the cheapest of paper, even wrapping paper or newsprint, making them difficult to preserve.)

Although forbidden to display his work publicly, Zverev gradually won the attention of other admirers and other sponsors. In the opinion of George Costakis and some other experts, Zverev's best work was created during the decade from 1955 to 1965. After that productive period he led an increasingly unregulated life, and his work became less remarkable, though he continued to find purchasers. He died in 1986 at the age of 55.

Zverev's work now sells on the international market, and the works of this "underground painter" are exhibited in Russian galleries and museums. In the art world Zverev is recognized as one of the principal representatives of the Russian Expressionist movement of the mid-twentieth century.

A small book of reproductions of some Zverev paintings and drawings was published in 1994, with an introduction and commentary by the compiler, Saveli Yamschikov, and with additional comments by fellow-artist Sergei Kuskov, as well as lengthy quotations from George Costakis (*Anatoli Zverev: Albom.* Avtor-sostavitel Saveli Yamschikov. Moskva, Izdatelstvo Galart, 1994).

Some references to Zverev's life and character also occur in Peter Roberts's biography of George Costakis, mentioned above.

CANADA/RUSSIA SERIES

CRCR

First Foreign Posting is set in Cartier and printed on Rolland Opaque Vellum, Natural.
The cover is printed on Cornwall Coated Card.

PENUMBRA PRESS
www.penumbrapress.ca